DC-3
courtesy AussieAirlines, Bob Smith

COME FLY WITH ME ... ON A DC-3

"Better five minutes late than dead on time!"

Displayed in the Brisbane TAA Pilot's Crew Room

JOY ALLARDYCE

First published by Ultimate World Publishing 2019
Copyright © 2019 Joy Allardyce

ISBN

Paperback - 978-1-925884-87-6
Ebook - 978-1-925884-88-3

Joy Allardyce has asserted her right under the Copyright, Designs and Patents Act 1988 to be identified as the author of this work. The information in this book is based on the author's experiences and opinions. The publisher specifically disclaims responsibility for any adverse consequences, which may result from use of the information contained herein. Permission to use information has been sought by the author. Any breaches will be rectified in further editions of the book.

All rights reserved. No part of this publication may be reproduced, stored in or introduced into a retrieval system, or transmitted in any form, or by any means (electronic, mechanical, photocopying, recording or otherwise) without the prior written permission of the author. Any person who does any unauthorised act in relation to this publication may be liable to criminal prosecution and civil claims for damages. Enquiries should be made through the publisher.

Cover design: Ultimate World Publishing
Layout and typesetting: Ultimate World Publishing
Editor: Hayley Ward

Ultimate World Publishing
Diamond Creek,
Victoria Australia 3089
www.writeabook.com.au

Dedication

For all the dedicated and resilient Air Hostesses who crewed the intrepid DC-3 aircraft in Queensland and other states during the early 1950's and beyond.

"One consolation of ageing is realising that while you have been growing old your friends haven't been standing still in the matter either."

Clare Boothe Luce

Contents

Dedication v
Prologue ix
Introduction xi
Chapter 1: The DC-3 1
Chapter 2: On Looking Back 3
Chapter 3: Training 5
Chapter 4: The Face of TAA 15
Chapter 5: First DC-3 Flight Ex Brisbane 19
Chapter 6: A Queensland Western 25
Chapter 7: Silver Service On The DC-3 VH-AEQ ... 35
Chapter 8: Brisbane - Darwin 39
Chapter 9: Charter Flight - 1963 45
Chapter 10: Innisfail Emergency Landing VH-AEQ 47
Chapter 11: Not A Hostess On This Flight 51
Chapter 12: The Chunderbus 55
Chapter 13: New Guinea DC-3 Adventures 59
Chapter 14: A Hostess In Flight Mode 63
Chapter 15: TAA Memories 67
Chapter 16: Qantas New Guinea Reminiscing 71

Chapter 17: Memories Of Ansett-ANA Days....................79
Chapter 18: Taxi!..81
Chapter 19: Not Always A Bed Of Roses!.......................83
Chapter 20: Townsville Duty...99
Chapter 21: Tyre Blowout..105
Chapter 22: Dust Storm Over New South Wales 109
Chapter 23: Tricks Of The Trade 113
Chapter 24: A Four-day Western 119
Chapter 25: I Copped The Lot! 125
Chapter 26: The Convair CV-240 127
Chapter 27: Winter Months 131
Chapter 28: The Russian Built DC-3 – Lisunov li-2.....133
Chapter 29: Wings Away (Qld) Inc 135
Author..139
Acknowledgements...141

Prologue

Queensland 1953

We were on the return leg of flight 486/487 Mount Isa, Cloncurry, Julia Creek, Richmond, Hughenden, Charters Towers, Townsville after leaving Mount Isa at 0630 (6.30am). It was mid-January, and the summer heat was intense. The DC-3 was continually buffeted by updrafts fed by the ground heat and passengers were not travelling well.

Descending into Hughenden on the hop from Richmond the turbulence increased, so I checked that everyone was wearing seatbelts in compliance with the "Fasten Seatbelt" sign switched on by the Captain. If the "No Smoking" sign had also been activated, I too would need to be strapped in. However, I was standing at the rear of the cabin, keeping an eye on the passengers when a man in a forward seat stood up.

He stumbled towards me clinging to the seats as his body swayed with the motion of the aircraft – I assumed he was heading to the lavatory. When he drew level with me and we were face-to-face, I asked, "Can

COME FLY WITH ME ... ON A DC-3

I help you?" He opened his mouth to speak, but unfortunately, no words escaped just a steady stream of vomit! I copped the lot!

"Please be seated," I gasped, "we will be landing soon. There are sick bags in the pocket of the seat in front of you."

Without a word, he turned and staggered back to his seat.

A bottle of soda water partially cleaned my uniform, even so, the smell lingered for the remainder of the flight and the tram ride home.

Introduction

*"Go confidently in the direction of your dreams.
Live the life you've imagined."*
Henry David Thoreau

So much has changed in the aviation industry since 1952. Larger, faster aircraft bring overseas destinations within reach of all Australians who have the travel bug. We no longer have Air Hostesses (hosties), they have become Flight Attendants, and passengers' dress mode has fallen from stylish fashions for females and suits with shirt and tie for males (except for destinations such as Darwin or Northern Queensland when just a shirt and tie sufficed) into casual wear.

These days we are more inclined to see passengers wearing jeans and shorts complemented by the dreaded flip flops which are great for the beach but somewhat irksome and unattractive for aircraft travel. At least in the case of an emergency ditching in the ocean, we would not have to worry about spiked heels penetrating the exit chute or the life raft!

I hope you, the reader, will enjoy these stories of the early Air Hostesses and the intrepid DC-3. How lucky I was to be able to see this vast, stunning land of ours; how lucky to make such wonderful friends and meet people from different states, different walks of life and different countries all because of the "good old DC-3 days".

This book is motivated by all the wonderful memories I have of those heady flying days and the long-lasting friendships formed while flying in Queensland and southern states, including Tasmania, as well as the Northern Territory.

It is written with pride for an organisation that reached so many people, not only those on or near the eastern seaboard but also those resilient souls who lived in the Outback regions where isolation can be likened to living on an island. Instead of the surrounding ocean lapping at the shoreline or damaging, ferocious cyclones that tear at trees and demolish buildings, nature conjures up destructive dust storms and swirling willy-willies that breathe red dust over everything that stands in their path. These resourceful Outback people have big hearts while their homesteads and towns are simply microscopic dots in the vast land that encompasses their boundaries.

Trans-Australia Airlines (TAA), a government-owned organisation, the trading name of the Australian National Airlines Commission, commenced operation in February 1946. In June of that year, wrote Sir Hudson Fysh in his book "Wings to the World," Lester Brain began work as General Manager with John Borthwick as his personal assistant and Doug Laurie on the traffic side. Three months later, TAA's first flight was made on a DC-3 from Melbourne to Sydney.

On the 2nd April 1949, in Brisbane, TAA acquired the Queensland and Northern Territory Aerial Services (Qantas) routes serviced by Qantas Empire Airways (QEA) and this acquisition also included the Flying Doctor Service, now known as the Royal Flying Doctor Service (RFDS).

Fast forward 46 years to the 9th September 1992, when there was a re-enactment of TAA's first flight.

INTRODUCTION

DC-3 VH-AES 'HAWDON' on tarmac boarded by passengers 9th September 1992

Photograph of the re-enactment of TAA's first flight, courtesy of Brian Griffin who was a passenger on the flight, having worked for TAA for many years.

COME FLY WITH ME ... ON A DC-3

Left Joy Allardyce (Shipway) Right Fleur Hanley (Bradbury) outside the house at Elsternwick.

"I just love this photo. What a treasure it is. The uniform is wonderful. Don't they look like two lovely girls setting off on a great adventure?" Gabrielle Cash (2018).

And that is what it was, a "great adventure" from start to finish.

CHAPTER 1

The DC-3

"Wherever you go, go with all your heart."
Confucius

That incredible flying machine, the DC-3, sometimes called the Gooney Bird, has carried thousands of passengers and me safely over countless land and sea miles. The respect I have for this intrepid aeroplane and the pilots who fly it is total. Those of you who have been a passenger will know what I mean when I say "it promoted a close affinity to nature".

Most of my working time as an Air Hostess (hostie) was spent flying in Queensland when the DC-3 bumped its way across the Outback or battled its way through storms that pounded the coast during cyclone season. That was when hosties worked single-handed and didn't belong to a union!

During flight in the summer months, there was the incessant buffeting, the sudden air pocket jolt and hawks that sometimes got in the way.

COME FLY WITH ME ... ON A DC-3

On the ground, there was the harsh heat, the dust, the flies and quite often plagues of huge brown grasshoppers, plump from pickings clinging to clothes with such determined tenacity that pulling them free was a nefarious nightmare.

Despite these setbacks, I felt 'at home' working on the DC-3. It was to me a dependable aircraft, and I always felt safe no matter what the circumstances. Besides, the pilots who flew the DC-3 also had my complete trust for most of them were ex-Royal Australian Air Force (RAAF) from World War II.

That courageous aviatrix Nancy Bird Walton, in her book "My God! It's a Woman," had this to say after she met "that genius of aviation", Donald Douglas.

"His DC-3 was the workhorse of the world. During WWII it was affectionately known as the Dakota and was used as a troop carrier, supply ship and anything else that was necessary."

CHAPTER 2

On Looking Back

"Memory is the diary that we all carry about with us."

Oscar Wilde

There is a part of my life that lives eternally in my heart – happy years, adventurous years, the years of discovering my ability to overcome challenges that continually presented themselves when least expected. It was a time of growing up, of realising the intrinsic nature of friendships and believing in myself. It was my time spent working as an Air Hostess with the domestic airline Trans-Australia Airlines (TAA).

Memory is like a hidden treasure chest; it waits patiently for the key to be turned by some stimulating arousal – a voice, a smell, a song, or perhaps a photograph. We have all experienced this wonderful personal journey, no need for me to elaborate.

COME FLY WITH ME ... ON A DC-3

When the title, COME FLY WITH ME ... ON A DC-3 popped into my head, there flashed before me a shifting scene of mercurial memories. My mind did somersaults, and my soul ran riot through the kaleidoscope of past events, while now and then, it focused on a special moment frozen in time, and I paused to savour the memory.

Today I am cruising down memory lane and treading the road that leads to a secret place. Now I'm surfing the waves of happenings that passed in another time and yay, there they are waiting to be reborn, re-felt and enjoyed once more!

Of course, there is some sorrow too, but today I am not dwelling on negatives. Instead, I close that door, and there they must stay forever or, until one day, the door springs open when touched by a present-day provocation, like a grain of sand that irritates an oyster.

CHAPTER 3
Training

"Many people will walk in and out of your life, but only true friends will leave footprints in your heart."
Eleanor Roosevelt

When I joined TAA as a trainee Air Hostess, we had two months of intensive instruction, both theoretical and practical. Part of our education included learning the registration name and type of aircraft of which there were 42. The names were usually explorers, so they were familiar, having learned about them in Australian history at school – the hard part was matching up the VH registration number with a name. Needless to say, by the time our examinations loomed, we were really pushing to remember them all, plus everything else.

In a rare mood of gaiety, the TAA "powers that be" placed 12 of our 13-member School 52 into a beautiful two-storey home on Gladstone Parade in the Melbourne suburb of Elsternwick There we lived in a sort of controlled chaos sharing two bathrooms - one upstairs and one downstairs - five bedrooms, lots of laughter and the inevitable anxiety associated with end-of-course examinations, some written others practical. What fun we had, a time in my life that I would gladly do all over again!

Our School 52 consisted of four girls from New South Wales, four from Queensland and four from South Australia. The Victorian member elected to live at home. At first, we sat in "States" for meals. The huge kitchen had three cubicles that each seated four to six persons, but it was not long before we were all chatting and sharing our hopes for the coming months of training. We also shared a few jokes!

It was an ideal situation for studying and being able to discuss a problem with the other girls helped a great deal. Every morning we exited the house, sometimes in single file depending on our wake-up call and the availability of the bathroom! It must have intrigued the neighbours, especially when we graduated, and we were wearing uniform. "Hey, wait for me!" was a familiar call.

Our lectures were varied. Aircraft components, cabin procedures, make-up, deportment, caring for babies during flight, necessary paperwork for each flight, airsick passengers and our general behaviour both on and off the aircraft, particularly while in uniform. Captain Frank Fisher explained what would happen in the event of a crash landing on land such as a beach or what to expect if we were involved in a ditching in the ocean. How to prepare the passengers – pens out of pockets, shoes off in case the exit chute or life raft was punctured by a spiked heel, shoulders and head forward towards the back of the seat in front, and life vests were carried under seats when we flew over ocean on the way to Tasmania. In the case of an emergency, it was imperative that we made sure everyone was wearing one, and it was fitted correctly. I remember thinking, "I hope we have time for all of this." Captain Fisher also told us in the event of ditching the pilots had their own escape route while we took care of the passengers. We all laughed at that, a sort of relief after the seriousness of the talk. Then we had a lecture on take-off and landing, and it was all intensely interesting.

TRAINING

During this time, we worked several training flights with a senior hostie and mine was a quietly-spoken, super-efficient hostie. I only had her for two flights then another senior Hostess took over, her name was Alwyn, a beautiful lady with red hair and a sunny disposition. I had a lot of fun, in the best possible way, learning the essentials of crewing a DC-3.

In the early 1950's we flew out of Essendon Airport, Melbourne, which was entirely different from the modern-day flights out of bustling Tullamarine Airport. It was much more relaxed, and we were like one big family, all working towards the same goal. On training flights, passengers often asked why I was not wearing a uniform as we wore civilian clothes with a TAA badge displayed so that people were aware that we were part of the team. The badges were surrendered when we graduated and received our uniforms, half wings, nameplate and Diplomas.

We also had "cabin" training in a DC-3, which was parked in the hangar. While one trainee acted out the role of an Air Hostess during flight, the others in the class acted as the passengers. It was a great way to learn – no cabin noise, no bumps – all plain sailing!

I have a confession to make – on my first training flight in 1952 which was Melbourne, Canberra, Sydney return, I felt ill while flying over the mountains before landing in Canberra. It was a mixture of excitement, erratic tail movements and the pungent odour of scotch eggs which were on the breakfast menu.

Oh, my goodness, the smell that assailed me when the door was closed and locked, and we were taxiing out to the runway. It was certainly unfamiliar and odious to my sense of smell, however, it improved somewhat when there was a rush of air through the vents, but I continued to feel queasy, so I requested permission to sit down. "No!" my training hostie responded, "keep moving, and it will go away." She was right, I kept working, and I never felt like throwing up again.

COME FLY WITH ME ... ON A DC-3

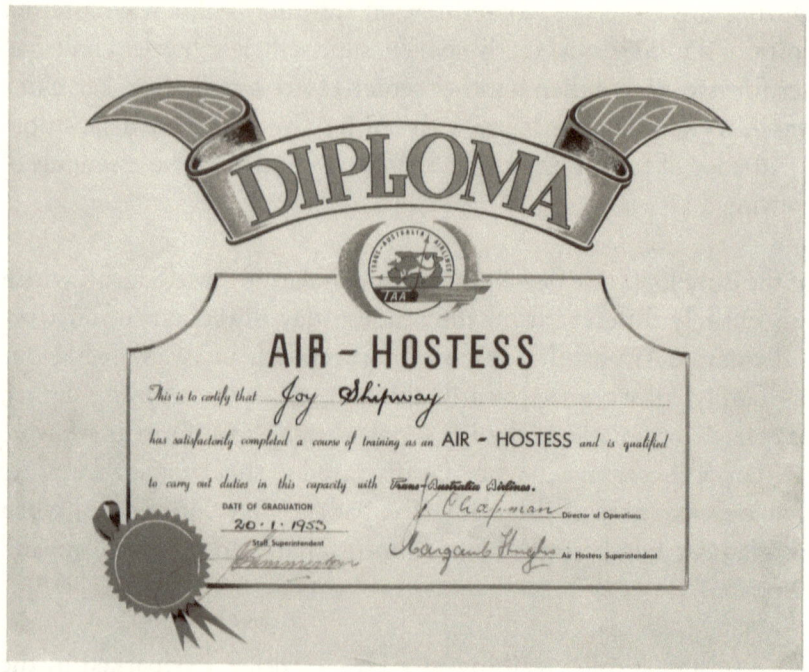

TAA Diploma - Joy Allardyce (Shipway) 20th January 1953

Flying over mountains can be turbulent, and I hadn't yet found my 'flying legs' so arrival at Mascot Airport, Sydney was a blessing, and when the Traffic Officer opened the door, the onslaught of fresh air was like a tonic. My parents were standing behind the fence opposite the aircraft, and after the passengers had disembarked, I requested permission to leave the aircraft and say hello. "You have five minutes only," said my training hostess, frowning her displeasure. "This is a turn-around flight; you need to be checking." My mother told me years later that when the aircraft door opened, this white face appeared – me. The return flight was not so rough, and my legs were feeling as though they belonged to me. I had survived without needing a sick bag! Another challenge behind me.

One thing I cannot forget is the distinctive odour that permeated the cabin after the aircraft had stood at the edge of the strip under the fierce western sun. A nauseous cocktail of metal, food, disinfectant, vomit,

TRAINING

heat and cigarette smoke. Extremely unpleasant for the passengers but accepted with alacrity by most hostesses as "just part of the job." One young lady I was training, ex Brisbane, was so ill on each of her training flights, she decided that flying was not for her.

However, I must admit that when I resigned from TAA, feeling sad and with a heavy heart, it was a very long time before I enjoyed a chicken salad, many years before tinned peaches tempted my palette, and I have never eaten scotch eggs or tinned fruit salad since.

A friend of mine, Jan Brennan (deceased), a British Airways (BA) ex hostie had a flatmate from England visiting, and we heard lots of amusing stories about flights from England to America, although not on DC-3s. Something the visitor said stuck in my mind, "you will always be my friend, dear Jan because you know too much about me."

And, that is how it was, these wonderful young ladies with whom I shared the Melbourne house and later, Mavis Beall (Holmes), Del Pellow (Wilesmith) and Fay Lambert (Goodger) in Brisbane became the sisters I never had – confidantes of the highest order, and that bond continues today between those of us who are still around to enjoy it. The camaraderie that exists between us has been tested by the passage of time and by the separation of land and sea miles, but it is as robust as ever, so I think we can safely say that it will last forever.

I remember after one of my early morning Melbourne flights, walking exhausted into a coffee lounge, sinking into a chair with a magazine and asking the waitress for a cup of white coffee. She stared at me strangely and said, "we don't serve coffee here". I peered around the sparsely-furnished room, and everyone had a glass of wine on the table in front of them. Melbourne had these little shops in lanes that resembled coffee shops, but in reality, they were wine saloons. This surprised me, but I didn't loiter. As I bolted out of the room clutching the magazine, gloves, handbag, shoes half on and forgetting about my aching feet, I could visualise myself being hauled up in front of the Superintendent and being asked for an explanation. Dismissal could be on the agenda! Under no circumstances, while in uniform, were we allowed to consume alcohol or smoke in public places. From that day on, every coffee shop was subjected to a thorough reconnoitre before entering.

The news of my posting to Brisbane port came soon after graduation, and after being checked by our School Supervisor on a return Hobart flight, I was the first of *School 52* to be posted. I was elated as Brisbane had been my first choice but the Queensland girls who had also requested Brisbane were bitterly disappointed.

The following is a poem written by a friend. He wrote it when we received our postings, and we treasure it. Every time I read his words, I have to smile because as each hostie is mentioned, I see them standing before me as they were when we first met in October 1952.

TRAINING

THE TWELVE AT TWENTY-THREE

Before this gifted class
Starts to break up –alas,
I'd like to paint a lass
Men would pick from the mass.

This near-perfect female
In whom each male will hail
The image of his love,
For attributes will have.

First the nose of Pauline,
Next the smile of Doreen,
Of Quinn, Mary the cheek,
Of gay Patsy the squeak,
Mavis's searing eyes,
Joy's Junoesque size,
Pamela's swinging hips,
Judy's appealing lips,
Maggie's bewitching wile,
Young Fleur's enchanting guile,
Jean's look for a teaser
Like famed Mona Lisa
Lastly to mix it well
The impishness of Del.

Joe Harari
12-12-52

COME FLY WITH ME ... ON A DC-3

School 52 Graduation Day
Courtesy of THE ARGUS January 1953

TRAINING

School 52 Hostess Examinations
Courtesy of *THE ARGUS* January 1953
L – R Joy Allardyce (Shipway), Mavis Beall (Holmes),
Patsy Booth (Sedgwick), Dell Pellow (Wilesmith) and
Fleur Hanley (Bradbury)

CHAPTER 4

The Face of TAA

My second training flight was traumatic for me. We were crewing a Melbourne/Adelaide return, departing Melbourne during the afternoon and arriving in Adelaide around 1830 (6:30 pm). The flight was fully booked, mostly businessmen returning home and it was busy – no time to feel sick! The DC-3 cabin seemed stretched to its limit, and the hat rack crammed full of briefcases, suit coats and men's hats, the passengers stuffing carry on objects into every available space.

At last, the passengers were seated, and the Traffic Officer completed his paperwork with the pilots and a headcount with us. All good. The cabin door slammed shut as the words, "have a good flight" echoed through the cabin.

Time to offer barley sugar and magazines before take-off while the DC-3 bumps gently out to the runway. For me, walking the aisle while the senior hostie attends to paperwork is uphill and downhill until the aircraft levels at cruising height. And don't forget I am not yet wearing a uniform, but I have purchased a pair of court shoes with moderate heels.

COME FLY WITH ME ... ON A DC-3

Since two hosties are working the flight, we have time to spare, so my training hostess takes me through a few pertinent issues making sure I am well versed in rules and regulations. At Adelaide Airport, we disgorge our passengers, all eager to be on the way home, and begin the process of checking catering being loaded and making sure the cabin is once again in a pristine condition. Then we hear the flight call, and passengers start heading out. We stand at the door greeting each passenger, checking their tickets for flight number and advising them where their seat is situated in the cabin.

One of the first things we learned as a trainee hostess was that a welcome smile always helped those passengers who might be nervous or anxious to feel at ease and no matter what the circumstances, to smile was extremely important, for we were the 'FACE OF TAA'. *During training, our School Supervisor continually emphasised that people would judge TAA by our attention to their comfort, not just for half an hour but for the whole length of the flight.* Once again, the flight is fully booked, and the racks packed to capacity with carry-on gear. There is an atmosphere of congenial chatter as everyone settles and then -- the bombshell! The Traffic Officer tells us that I am to be offloaded and will spend an overnight in Adelaide. I had done the unforgivable; I had come without an overnight bag. During training, we had been warned about the Melbourne/Adelaide afternoon flight because of heavy loading and told we should always carry an overnight bag. I had been caught out – for me, a lesson learned the hard way!

Traffic Officers are always helpful. They organised hotel accommodation and sent a message to my housemates in Melbourne, explaining that I was delayed overnight and would be home sometime the next day. Then they arranged transport for me into Adelaide.

The receptionist at the hotel told me that there would be a crew arriving later that evening and she would make sure they knew I would be returning with them to the airport in the morning. She gave me a room opposite the crew so that I would know when they arrived and could introduce myself, which I did. They were sympathetic with my predicament, and I flew back to Melbourne supernumerary with them the next morning. The flight crew were Captain John Benton and First Officer Ernest Luder DFC, who later died in a tragic Vampire jet fighter accident. I remember an eyewitness saying that he gave his life to save crashing into houses.

Through my lack of forethought and inattention to sound advice during training, my housemates learned a lesson the easy way!

CHAPTER 5

First DC-3 Flight Ex Brisbane

"They are able who think they are able."
Virgil, 70-19BC Roman Poet

I landed at Eagle Farm Airport, Brisbane, in January 1953 after travelling supernumerary from Essendon, Melbourne. When travelling supernumerary, we wore our uniform, either summer or winter depending on the season, and had to wait until all the passengers had boarded before we could embark. If the aircraft was fully loaded, permission from the Captain was required to travel in the jump seat in the cockpit. This was an interesting adventure as we were privy to the pre-take-off and pre-landing procedures carried out by the pilots. TAA had booked me into a hotel in The Valley, and the manager's wife took me under her wing by not allowing me to sleep during the afternoon's steamy heat, plus there were other flight crew members staying there, so it was a friendly atmosphere in which I found myself.

COME FLY WITH ME ... ON A DC-3

A few weeks later, members from the course joined me and we ultimately found and shared a house which proved to be a long tram ride from the city and a long walk from the tram to the house, which didn't help my aching feet after a tiring day, however, it was fun and we all bonded extremely well, in fact we are still friends.

Flights were much longer ex Brisbane, but the staff and passengers were easy-going, and I soon settled down although not without a couple of mishaps. Crewing the DC-3 was arduous and due to the summer heat acclimatisation came slowly, although initiation was quick. I was on my own right from the start!

One flight that lingers forever in my mind is the early morning Brisbane-Cairns flight which covered the eastern seaboard. Ports of call were Maryborough, Rockhampton, Mackay, Proserpine, Ayr, Townsville, Innisfail, Cairns. It was a tiring flight, but TAA had a hostel in Cairns that catered for crews, so we were well looked after on overnights enjoying the tasty home-cooked meals prepared by a lovely lady who was the housekeeper. It was far better than hotel accommodation, and we were able to relax. I still cannot forget the large green frog that took up residence in our downstairs lavatory. He blew bubbles and after a flush clung to the side of the bowl with vigorous determination.

The Brisbane-Cairns overnight was the first flight I crewed ex Brisbane, and it really tested me since I was out of my comfort zone in-so-far as the flying was concerned.

On the DC-3's we carried large steel urns used for liquids and hot meals. They sat behind the rear seats in the tail and during the flight they had to be lifted from floor to buffet and back to the floor again before landing. They were heavy when filled with hot water or other liquids, so we needed plenty of strength to lift them. While taking off from Maryborough, on this particular occasion, one of the urns toppled over, startling the passengers and me. The lid flew off, and while I watched in horror, strapped into the hostess seat, tomato juice flooded the buffet floor and lapped around my feet!

FIRST DC-3 FLIGHT EX BRISBANE

Oh, my goodness, what a mess and no drain in the floor either. The movement in the tail was sending it swirling backwards and forwards like an ebbing tide. When the aircraft reached cruising height, I went up to the cockpit to explain the loud bang made by the urn as it hit the floor. The crew thought it was funny until my stricken face sobered their mirth, and the First Officer came back and helped me mop up with rags that we carried for such disasters. I was grateful for the help, and the remainder of the flight was uneventful.

I had written about this calamity in a short story "… and the Flights Headed West" published by the Sunday Mail magazine *COLOR*, December 16, 1979. After it appeared, I received a few letters from ex hosties who had experienced the same dilemma, but one from an ex Australian National Airlines (ANA) hostie wrote of her accident – instead of tomato juice, it was scrambled eggs! Imagine what that would be like to clean up. I judged scrambled eggs worse than tomato juice; I had the better deal.

During cyclone season we were often unable to land at Rockhampton and other coastal towns because of floods. Water spread everywhere and looking down from the aircraft the submerged mountain valleys looked like lakes. Landing in Cairns could be hazardous too because of the layout of the runway, ocean on three sides, a mountain on the fourth. If we happened to be caught in a rainstorm heading into Cairns, it sometimes meant spending lengthy periods of time while the pilots carried out an instrument landing, banking and circling, and as we descended the cabin heated and many passengers became ill. The aircraft lurched and swayed while buffeted by torrential rain squalls and visibility was negligible. Northern towns like Townsville had deep monsoon drains that were constructed to handle the copious amounts of rain that cascaded like impenetrable sheets of water and gushed through the drains until they resembled fast-moving rivers.

On another flight to Cairns, I had as a passenger our popular Brisbane-based check hostess, Irene (Davis). When I mentioned it to Fleur Hanley (Bradbury) who had arrived on a direct flight from Brisbane earlier and who would work the return flight the next day back to Brisbane, she worried most of the night in case she would be checked as well. I guess it was better not to know but to expect it kept you up to the mark.

That was the night we were in bed talking about our flights when I spied two black feelers edging around the chest of drawers between our beds followed by a huge black creepy-crawly, the like of which I had never seen before. It was ugliness personified!

I leapt out of bed ending up on the floor entangled in sheets, only to be told by a laughing Fleur, "It is only a cockroach!" After a couple of years living in Queensland, I became adept at squashing these prehistoric creatures so that they did not ooze mess all over the place, although sometimes they would rally and lumber off to recuperate in some unimaginable dark hole.

One night when I disturbed a large black cockroach feasting on the butter in the cupboard, I decided to accept them for what they were; a distinctly onerous household pest that was here to stay and my feeble efforts at annihilation did not make any difference to their population.

In Brisbane city in the early 1950s, there was an advertisement for a product used for killing cockroaches. Unfortunately, I am unable to remember the name. The advertisement was in the form of a large black cockroach, about two feet long, reclining on its back, hairy legs waving in the breeze. This hideous replica was on a trolley that was pulled along Queen Street by a man. A blessing they did not grow to that size in real life, but I always chuckled when I saw it for that is how they ended up when they died – on their backs with legs in the air.

Sometimes on return flights from Cairns or Townsville, the Proserpine agent gave me a cylindrical box (about 12 inches tall) full of frozen oysters. Wow! They were the largest I had ever seen except for those served for breakfast on Orpheus Island. When I lived at home in Sydney, my father often came home on Friday night with prawns and Sydney rock oysters but nothing like the size of those the agent gave me.

FIRST DC-3 FLIGHT EX BRISBANE

There was another Brisbane-Cairns flight I enjoyed because after landing in Townsville we transferred to a Lockheed Lodestar aircraft which was smaller but faster than the DC-3. It seated 11 passengers and did not have a buffet for food preparation, so we carried lunch in boxes – an easy flight. As far as I can remember, there were only three pilots who were endorsed to fly the Lodestar and take-off could be dangerous because the luggage was loaded in the nose. One of the pilots was very tall, and I can remember him sort of folding his legs into the small cockpit.

COME FLY WITH ME ... ON A DC-3

Joy Allardyce (Shipway) in uniform for the first time

CHAPTER 6

A Queensland Western

"Better five minutes late than dead on time."

So, come fly with me on a Queensland western and experience the DC-3's tenacity. We will skip your training; you can do that later. Today you are my shadow.

I am crewing an early morning return flight, pick up 0430 hours (4.30am). Departure time 0630 (6.30am). While others sleep, we make our way to Eagle Farm Airport collecting the ground hostess, pilots and hostesses crewing the early morning flights. The Brisbane pre-dawn is the best part of the day during summer months, at least the air is cool and not so clingy. Conversation is scarce in the pick-up as we are all resting before the day begins.

You will notice that I am wearing a grey uniform, identical to our summer white one; however, a more serviceable colour since western flights can be messy! I have polished my buttons, buckle and half wings. I have checked that my stocking seams are straight, I have polished my shoes – uniform demands we wear navy blue court shoes with a moderate heel. It would not only be hilarious teetering around the cabin in high heels but also hazardous while riding the bumps. My navy-blue hat sits at the correct angle over the right eye; I have my navy-blue cotton gloves and navy handbag. Makeup not too heavy since the higher you fly, the lighter the light, therefore the harsher the make-up appears. Since I am wearing my grey uniform, there is no need for me to wear the obligatory neutral shades of undergarments and half petticoat, which is a rule when wearing our white summer uniform.

Are you, my shadow, ready to go?

Come follow me as I sign the Flight Crew book half an hour before take-off (as is required). Inside the brightly-lit airport lounge still smelling faintly of yesterday's heat, the Traffic Officers are busy with tickets and weighing luggage while passengers loiter around eager to be on the way. Outside a pale dawn streaks the sky and soon the sun will begin another day's journey.

Follow me as I board the aircraft, making sure I have the correct one as there are three standing on the apron. The catering crew are busy finishing installing the food and with a quick "hello," I set to work checking and signing paperwork.

Trays, food, cutlery, serviettes (paper), sugar, coffee, tea, milk, salt and pepper shakers, barley sugar, hot water (in urn), cold water (in urn), tomato juice (in urn). Next the bar – those cute miniature bottles of spirits. Also, beer and soft drinks - mainly soda water, ginger ale and lemonade. We need to carry small currencies for the bar, no tipping allowed.

Check urns are safely secured, lids tightly fastened. Food is served in blue plastic tableware, unbreakable and light in weight.

I sign off on all the documents, and the catering crew depart.

A QUEENSLAND WESTERN

During checking the Captain and the First Officer board the aircraft and the Captain asks, "Good morning, Joy, all ready for the flight?"

"Yes, all ready", I reply, but I am thinking "your flight will be better than mine, the cockpit is a more stable ride."

The pilots slide their plastic nameplates into the slots provided on the right-hand side of the bulkhead. Mine slips into the third slot beneath the First Officer's name. There is also a place for the Captain's Flight Log that is passed to passengers during the flight, giving them pertinent information concerning the flight.

Ground speed, airspeed, outside temperature, height above sea level, name of aircraft, flight, destination, tailwind or headwind, ETA (Estimated Time of Arrival), the date and remarks.

Next chore is to check the cabin: magazines, pillows, rugs, headrests, sick bags in pockets at the back of seats and in the lavatory. Check hat racks in case an article has been left from a previous flight, fire extinguisher and ashtrays.

All of this can be done at a glance, but one of the most important items is the old-fashioned tin opener – the stab can opener – the one with the pointed tip like a cocky's beak that needs to be "stabbed" into the tin's lid with as much force as possible while being flung around by the unpredictable tail movements. It often leaves a bruise on the palm of my hand so I think perhaps a hammer would be a better proposition! Tinned peaches and tinned fruit salad were very popular with catering and necessary on our four-day trips as they did not need refrigeration.

Did you notice that the DC-3 stands at an angle on the tarmac so before take-off and after landing I am walking uphill and downhill? When the aircraft reaches cruising height, it levels. Unfortunately for the passengers and for me, if ports of call only have short hops in between landings, we fly lower, and this is when turbulence is greatest, especially during summer months

COME FLY WITH ME ... ON A DC-3

I hear the flight boarding call over the loudspeaker. Passenger's tickets are checked at the lounge gate by the ground hostess who directs them to the correct aircraft. I wait at the aircraft door to welcome the passengers and check their tickets again, not forgetting to smile a good morning greeting before directing them to their seats. There are seven rows of double seats on the port side facing the nose and seven rows of single seats on the starboard, 21 passengers in all. The hostess seat is behind the starboard passenger seats.

The manifest shows a full complement plus two pilots and one cabin crew. It also gives me the names and seat numbers of each passenger in case I need to speak to one during the flight. When everyone has boarded, and cabin carry-on luggage is stored in overhead racks, the Traffic Officer boards and proceeds to the cockpit for last-minute checking. I make a headcount, and this must tally with the Traffic Officer's paperwork.

Sometimes a passenger is late or has inadvertently boarded the wrong aircraft, however, during my flying time that disaster never happened to me although I did hear of an incident where a bridegroom ex Adelaide boarded the Melbourne-bound aircraft in lieu of the Sydney aircraft. Luckily for everyone in that instance, he was found at the last minute and was able to transfer just before his flight departed.

In the early 1950s flying was much more relaxed, and Captains often waited for a passenger even though this particular passenger had to sprint across the tarmac. Since he was unaware that his luggage had already been loaded onto the Sydney bound aircraft, he was heard shouting as he raced across the tarmac "My luggage! My luggage! Don't forget my luggage!" Would such a disaster as this cause embarrassment and repercussions for the hosties? Oh, yes! Imagine the bride's wrath, too, if the groom landed in Melbourne in lieu of Sydney!

All good today – headcount tallies. The Traffic Officer closes the door after a wave and "Have a good flight." I check to make sure the door is locked! The FASTEN SEATBELT sign and the NO SMOKING sign light up on the starboard side of the bulkhead. While the pilots check the engines, you and I will make sure that the passengers are buckled up. I offer barley sugar – continual swallowing on take-off in an unpressurised aircraft helps clear the ears. For babies and young children sucking on a bottle of water helps. We are ready to go, and we are on time.

Strap up and come fly with me. Since the hostess seat is at the rear, you and I will have a good view of the cabin to make sure no one stands up or lights up. If a passenger walks around during take-off, the movement alters the aircraft's trim. You would be surprised at the number of people who decide they need the restroom on take-off or perhaps a cigarette to calm the nerves. Smoking during both take-off and landing is a definite "No! No!" and never allowed in the lavatory.

We begin taxiing, and that is when I feel the anticipated thrill of the flight ahead, for every day is different. One of my pleasures once airborne is being able to have a close encounter with clouds, particularly cumulus clouds, so beautiful in their bulbous formations, and they always remind me of cotton wool. Sometimes I feel like jumping into them!

While we taxi, I check the paperwork which is pretty mundane, but it has to be done. The DC-3 bounces gently until we reach the end of the designated runway where it turns ready for take-off. One by one the engines roar then a final burst together and soon we are moving, slowly at first, gradually building up speed, and I watch the ground rushing past through the rear window. Now we are airborne, a clonk as the wheels retract (100 feet from the ground is a danger zone), and we climb, and fresh air flows in through the air vents. If a passenger complains about the cabin temperature, either too hot or too cold, I will attempt to regulate it, although the controls can be temperamental.

First port of call is Goondiwindi. When the aircraft levels, I begin the job ahead, serving breakfast, tea and coffee. There is no time for dilly-dallying and time passes quickly.

COME FLY WITH ME ... ON A DC-3

While descending in preparation for landing at the next port, I gather all the cups and magazines and tidy the buffet which is compact and easy to work in. Hot water urn back to the floor – we are not permitted to land with an urn on the buffet due to the fact that it could become a missile if we are experiencing turbulence. I secure the urn even though it is a struggle and takes all my strength to slip the tight elastic cord into the groove on the lid.

FASTEN SEATBELT sign and NO SMOKING sign light up, and I do a check of seatbelts while I hand out barley sugar. Come, it is time to buckle up and enjoy the landing. I can still savour the sensation of a three-point landing and the slight skid of wheels on touchdown.

Next port is St George, so it is just a repeat of the previous section, and the remainder of the flight (except for landing into Cunnamulla) is relatively calm, and I am able to serve refreshments without mishap. It will be a different story on the return flight.

Landing at Cunnamulla is smooth, and we taxi to where the passengers alight and I note the number of travellers waiting to board. I set about tidying the cabin and check the hot water and refreshments being loaded.

The agent takes care of the freight and baggage, and the pilots review the uplift weight. Unlike their southern counterparts or when working the coastal flights, the pilots wear khaki shirts and trousers and work hard during some western flights. They frequently load and unload baggage, newspapers, all types of freight or fresh produce when we call into station properties or small towns where business is conducted on the edge of a gravel or dirt strip.

Ex Cunnamulla I have 10 passengers – one is a lady with a baby about six months old. When she enters the cabin, I notice she is perspiring and anxious, not a good combination for the rough flight ahead. I decide to change her seat from the rear of the cabin in the tail to a front seat which is a more comfortable ride and allows more leg room. This is permitted if it is in the passenger's interest. I make a note in my report.

A QUEENSLAND WESTERN

The bumps begin not long after take-off and a couple of passengers are already clutching sick bags. The lady in the front seat joins them, so far baby is fine. It is remarkable how many people are often sick after touchdown and not during the flight. They will sit holding a bag looking decidedly pale and miserable for most of the flight then we land and I am glad they are prepared! A tell-tale sign that warns me if a passenger might be airsick is a white ring around the mouth. I keep a strict eye out for that – best to be prepared!

We land at St George and take on eight passengers. Unfortunately, the cabin is not smelling fresh despite the Airwick deodoriser. This is a common failing on western flights and is exacerbated while the aircraft is standing under the fierce sun.

You know the routine now. The sequence of checking might vary, but it all becomes routine, and problems can usually be detected easily. While we taxi out to the runway, I speak with the mother who confides that she is extremely nervous. She is perspiring again, so I give her a damp cloth to sponge her face. Once a passenger is ill, the smell permeates throughout the cabin and others will follow suit. A domino effect impossible to halt. Today is no exception.

The mother asks if I would give the baby, her name is Alice, a bottle, so I take the bub and the bottle of water, and we settle down for take-off. While Alice is drinking, she watches me with her big blue eyes that somehow seem older and wiser than her six months. When she is satisfied, she pushes the bottle away and sits up. She has been refuelled and is ready to rock. Not so poor Mum, so I tuck Alice under one arm and hang onto the rack with the other to steady myself as I check the passengers.

A lady who has a reprieve from being sick offers to take Alice while I collect sick bags for disposal. The receptacle for sick bags in the lavatory is crammed full, so I just throw the bag and hope for the best.

It is great to be airborne again, and fresh air flows through the vents; nevertheless, it is not long before each passenger is grasping a bag.

COME FLY WITH ME ... ON A DC-3

The tail is behaving like a bucking bronco, and I am suddenly caught unawares by an air pocket and am bent over by gravity for a few seconds. I try to swing the cold-water urn into position on the buffet but being thrown around by the tail's gyrations doesn't help. Thankfully, on the third swing, it connects. I offer cold water and dry ginger ale to the passengers – only a couple accept the offer. No food is served.

The next landing is the last port of call after leaving St George, and I now have a full aircraft to Brisbane. After take-off, we are immediately experiencing severe buffeting. The lady with the baby is dry retching, weak and exhausted, so I ask the Captain if he would radio Brisbane and request an ambulance to meet the aircraft. Now I am swapping with the passengers – a baby for a sick bag! Alice is having a great time.

I have just reached the cockpit door when suddenly, there is a loud bang. I turn back to investigate only to find an aisle floor panel has shaken loose and fallen into the fuselage below. We have a problem! I inform the Captain and then the passengers that when exiting the aircraft care must be taken in negotiating the gap in the floor. When we land, I sense great relief to be on the ground, so I pass out articles that have been stored in the overhead racks. We land with the same amount of refreshments that we took on board ex Cunnamulla plus the lavatory full of sick bags!

Time to say goodbye to the passengers as they disembark, smiling thinly from sallow faces. It was such a relief that Alice travelled well, not so poor Mum who is waiting for the ambulance officers. At last, she is in good hands, and they help her out and down the steps with baby paraphernalia spilling out of a quilted bag.

I begin checking and fill out the flight report noting all the extraordinary happenings, including loss of the aisle panel then leave everything else to the catering and cleaning crews.

This aircraft, despite continual buffeting, has carried us safely there and back. As I leave, I give the cabin an affectionate pat. I expect that after the aisle floor panel is replaced, this aircraft will be in the air again as soon as practical.

My day is almost over since I tumbled out of bed to the strident alarm this morning. We are not supposed to exceed 30 flying hours in a week – that does not take into consideration time spent on the ground checking before and after each flight plus time spent while freight, baggage and passengers unload and load at all the ports between Brisbane and our destination.

Did you travel well? I did, but I am feeling like a cuppa, a long soak in a bath and some pampering for my complaining feet.

"How foolish to think that one can ever slam the door in the face of age. Much wiser to be polite and gracious and ask him to lunch in advance."

Noel Coward

COME FLY WITH ME ... ON A DC-3

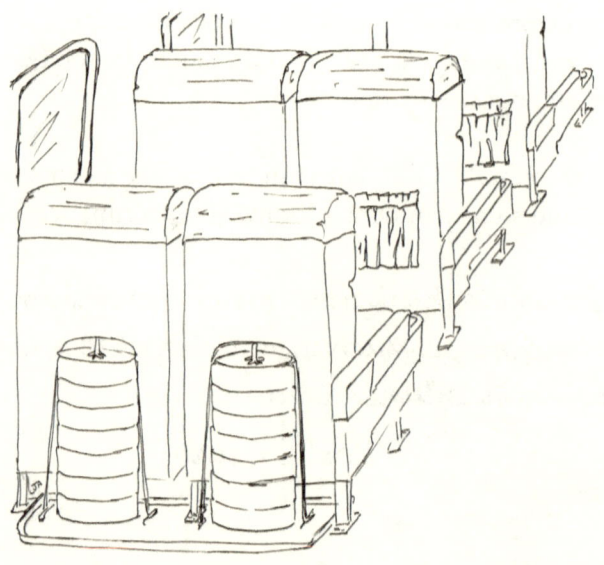

Sketch of urns by my daughter, Caroline Allardyce

CHAPTER 7

Silver Service On The DC-3 VH-AEQ

I was so excited to receive a call – "How would you like to do an 11-day charter on a DC-3 to New Guinea?" Well, I did not have to be asked twice! I had not been to New Guinea, so a whole new world of flying!

I met up with my 18 passengers in Cairns together with the tour leader, Mr Neville Salisbury. I did a double-take when I saw Neville. He looked to be all set to go on safari, complete with pith helmet. He explained to me that my role was to treat the passengers as VIPs and to make sure their flight was comfortable. Lunch trays on board were to be perfectly set up with white linen placemats, and crockery and glasses to be spotless! Well, that turned out to be a challenge. The passengers were of mature age except for two girls who were my age. The flights around the mountainous country were at times quite rough, and the two girls were happy to help with serving out the food, even to the point that they were thinking they would like to become air hostesses!

COME FLY WITH ME ... ON A DC-3

Our Captain was Larry Blackman, also known as Greasy for his great knowledge of the DC-3 and particularly his ability to grease the aircraft onto a runway with hardly a bump. Larry gained his experience in the RAAF during and after the war. We felt we were in really safe hands with Larry at the controls. We certainly felt we needed this reassurance as New Guinea is extremely rugged with mountains over twice as high as Mt Kosciusko. It was an absolute "no, no!" to fly into cloud in the Highlands of New Guinea because there was always a real possibility that the cloud might be full of mountain. Many of the airstrips were what was known as one-way strips where the aircraft landed up the slope and then took off back down again.

The passengers enjoyed the amazing scenery and Neville had done a wonderful job of organising interesting experiences such as "sing sings" at Banz in the Highlands, exploring the old gold mine at Bulolo and staying at the lodge poised on top of the mountain. We sailed on lakatois (outrigger canoes) and circled the volcanoes at Rabaul. It is a trip I will never forget, and this all happened in 1963!

The DC-3's were the mainstay of aviation in Papua New Guinea in the 1960's. They carried passengers throughout the territory, including native labour for the plantations and were known as BOI charters. They also carried almost everything as freight into the Highlands as at that time there were no reliable roads for trucks. The backloading from the Highlands included tea, coffee and other agricultural produce. Of course, our DC-3 was special as it had scenic windows and comfortable seating, unlike the rest of the DC-3 fleet which had side-saddle seats for high-density loading.

LAUREL FRASER
Ex TAA Air Hostess (1961-1964)

SILVER SERVICE ON THE DC-3 VH-AEQ

DC-3
courtesy AussieAirlines, Bob Smith

CHAPTER 8

Brisbane - Darwin

Brisbane, Longreach, Camooweal, Victoria River Downs Station, Tennant Creek, Katherine, Daly Waters, Darwin.

This flight was a favourite of mine even though it was approximately 12½ hours flying time plus checking time at the beginning and end of the flight. Add to that the time spent at the ports allowing passengers to disembark and board and freight to be loaded and unloaded. All together we were on the go for 16 hours.

The hops between towns on the Queensland leg of the trip gave us ample time to chat to the passengers and serve refreshments. Flights that covered the lunch hour usually carried chicken salads stored in separate slots on the buffet and we also carried sandwiches and biscuits.

Once we reached the Northern Territory, we had four landings ahead – Victoria River Downs, Tennant Creek, Katherine and Daly Waters where an aboriginal, very tall and always quick to smile carried our urn across the tarmac to replenish the hot water then carried it back to the aircraft. That would have been a real struggle for me, but he did it effortlessly.

We always saved the left-over sandwiches in the Northern Territory for the young aboriginal children who rushed over to say hello and clamber up the steps as soon as the door was opened. They liked barley sugar too – such happy smiles and lively chatter while their Mums watched from a distance. When we took off, they stood in a line and waved goodbye, probably planning what they would do when the next service landed.

It was a long day for us; nevertheless, it was worth the effort as we had four days off in Darwin staying at the luxurious Darwin Hotel owned by the Paspaley family. I made great friends up there, including the hairdresser at the hotel, who had a pet baby crocodile with snapping jaws and teeth like needles. I handled it very carefully! Also, two lovely Chinese girls who owned a milk bar which was very popular with the hosties and a young man who was the ABC reporter. On one of my trips, a group of us attended a formal ball at Berrimah, which was the Qantas stronghold. We travelled by bus and enjoyed a happy evening dancing and mopping perspiring faces! I was the lucky one; I was able to sleep in the next day.

Darwin in 1953 was an interesting city, a tropical paradise, with a cosmopolitan population of fascinating and often flamboyant characters. Underwater salvage experts, crocodile hunters, bank employees, doctors, nurses, a Royal Australian Naval Base and government employees. Everyone was friendly. I do remember a store that sold magnificent woven products, hats, mats, baskets, tablemats all made by aboriginal ladies who were very clever and creative. I took great pleasure in browsing the packed shelves that displayed the many hand-woven objects.

A few buildings, including the Bank of New South Wales that had been bombed during the Second World War (1939-1945) were still in their flattened state with steel rods poking out from the rubble, and

BRISBANE - DARWIN

the harbour was a graveyard for the many ships that had been sunk or damaged during air raids by Japanese aircraft.

The Darwin heat is humid and overpowering. November is called the suicide month and begins the build-up to the monsoon season with extremely vocal storms, lots of rumbling, ear-splitting thunderclaps while lightning flashes pierce the sky and light up the ominous, heavy storm clouds. The sultry heat envelopes the body like a wetsuit and sleep is almost impossible.

Some of the houses had inside partitions in lieu of walls so that they could be moved around the house and the exterior walls had lots of louvres that allowed the slats to be adjusted for a cool breeze or closed to shut out the torrential rain. Even so, I enjoyed my days in Darwin because it was different from other Australian cities and the nights softly ethereal.

On this flight, we departed Brisbane at first light which could vary according to the season, pick up 0300 (3:00am) arriving in Darwin around 1830 (6.30pm) South Australian time. The Brisbane pilots changed at Longreach and were replaced by a flight crew who had stayed overnight in Longreach from the previous day. This flight crew departed Darwin early next morning and again overnighted in Longreach while the pilots from the Brisbane/Longreach hop flew the aircraft back to Brisbane. It all sounds somewhat complicated since I am now going to say that the hostie in Darwin whom I would replace and who had completed her four days off crewed the return flight from Darwin to Brisbane.

Even though working on the DC-3 was strenuous I am glad I had the opportunity to see the Red Centre firsthand and to travel the Northern Territory in this intrepid aircraft. There is an aura about Australia's Centre, and it is certainly a place that grows on you. There is an enigma that cries out to be solved, but while it entices understanding, at the same time it remains strangely distant seemingly reticent to bare its soul. Perhaps by living there, one also becomes part of the land's ambiguous nature and therefore is enlightened as to its mystery.

COME FLY WITH ME ... ON A DC-3

I have seen hundreds of magnificent sunsets and sunrises from the window of a DC-3, but somehow the Northern Territory ones remain fixed in my memory as breathtakingly vibrant and undeniably romantic! Unfortunately, one can never quite capture on camera the spectacular fusion of colours as day drops out of sight, and our piece of earth is plunged into darkness. For me, the photograph does not evoke the same emotional response as the visual experience inspires. And, there is the infinite pleasure felt at being privy to the beauty of a molten sun seen slipping slowly from view leaving the night sky tinged with yellows, golds and orange hues. Then the glow gradually fades into amber, and in the blink of an eye, the horizon appears in stark contrast as though a brush dipped in purple paint has been dragged across the land. Suddenly, I feel sad that today's sunset is lost forever but glad that tomorrow there will be another, not identical but equally as beautiful.

One of the plus factors about the Brisbane/Darwin flight was that we cruised at 9,000 feet on the long hops and passengers tended to sleep. It was cold too, so everyone wrapped up in the rugs we carried, and I endeavoured to keep the cabin as warm as possible.

I experienced an odd incident on one of these hops. I was standing in the tail near the buffet enjoying a cup of coffee and watching the cabin when suddenly I heard bagpipes playing and immediately thought that the pilots had tuned into a radio station, although as it turned out, I was wrong. I guess it was a figment of my imagination because the DC-3 is unpressurised. Weird!

At that height, 9,000 feet, the air is rarefied, and I often felt breathless while working; however, we did carry oxygen which could be used if necessary. Of course, as we descended prior to landing the heat was upon us again, and while the aircraft stood on the tarmac waiting for passengers and freight to be loaded, we were once again sweltering.

It may appear that I complain endlessly about the heat, but it was not such a big problem once we acclimatised. And, I did enjoy crewing the DC-3; it has a special place in my heart.

BRISBANE - DARWIN

On one of my Darwin/Brisbane flights, I had a passenger, a sailor from the Darwin Naval Base, who was travelling to Brisbane for medical treatment. He insisted on showing me the wound, an ugly ulcer on his shin bone, that was proving difficult to manage in the moist Darwin environment. The conversation turned to our POW soldiers who were taken prisoner by the Japanese after the fall of Singapore in 1942. I had an Uncle who was captured and suffered ulcers and other tropical medical problems that became a formidable challenge since they were living in such horrific conditions. I lived in Malaysia for three years on Pulau Penang, so I am well aware of the humidity and heat the prisoners endured.

While in Darwin on my first flight, I made the mistake of going for a late afternoon swim at the protected pool just down from the Hotel. Next day I was covered from head to toe in sand-fly bites, so much so that at the end of my days off I had to request permission to work without stockings or my uniform hat because the lumps - the size of a ten-cent piece - were weeping. I was a mess; all I wanted to do was scratch! It turned out I had actually been poisoned. Mention sand-flies now and I run a mile!

At the Hotel, I often shared the room on a couple of nights of my stay with the TAA hostie from Adelaide who had flown up the Centre and the MacRobertson Miller Airlines (MMA) hostie from Perth. We called MMA 'Mickey Mouse' which brings to mind a saying we had in the early 50s and said with tongue in cheek of course:

TAA The Friendly Way

ANA The Family Way

Chance it with Ansett.

To all our wonderful ex hosties – no offence intended!

COME FLY WITH ME ... ON A DC-3

"We are made happy when reason can discover
no occasion for it.
The memory of some past moments is more
persuasive than the experience of present ones.
There have been visions of such breadth and brightness
that these motes were invisible in their light."

Signed Henry David Thoreau (1817 - 1862)
American writer and philosopher

CHAPTER 9
Charter Flight - 1963

Anna Elliott, third from right, 1963
Darwin Charter Flight showing passenger and flight crew

COME FLY WITH ME ... ON A DC-3

Letter from J Neville Salisbury

"To Anna,

With my very best wishes for your future and sincere personal thanks for the hard job well done.

J. Neville Salisbury
Australian Inland Air Charter Co. Pty. Ltd."

CHAPTER 10

Innisfail Emergency Landing VH-AEQ

I was so proud to be a TAA Air Hostess, having joined in August 1956, just before the Melbourne Olympics. When we arrived in Melbourne for training, it was bitterly cold, and our accommodation was also freezing with no heating, run down and dirty. Accommodation was so scarce with the Olympics commencing in November, but TAA did find alternative lodgings for us 13 girls of School 77. After one month of instruction and flying training, we were quickly posted to our allotted ports to finish our training. We all gathered back in Melbourne after the Olympics for Graduation Day in December, which has not left a lasting impression on me, unfortunately. No photos were taken in those days.

Flying in Queensland out of Brisbane port was hard work, enjoyable hard work. We regularly flew up the East Coast in our DC-3 aircraft landing at any or all of the following ports: Maryborough, Rockhampton, Mackay, Proserpine, Ayr, Townsville, Ingham, Innisfail and Cairns. We began flights in our starched white uniforms then returned early evening feeling so grubby and exhausted from the heat and the turbulence.

On the 8th July 1957, I was hostess on Flight 456 Brisbane/Cairns (all ports in between) in a DC-3, VH-AEQ and after leaving Townsville heading for Cairns and the hostel for a clean-up, rest and relaxation after the long day, Captain Bob Kirkby buzzed me to come to the cockpit. At first, I could not open the cockpit door, which puzzled me; however, the crew had a window open, so the air pressure made the door difficult to open. Captain Kirkby advised me that we were returning to Innisfail for an emergency landing because it had a grass strip. I took this in my stride and advised the passengers we were returning to Innisfail, which they took calmly. We landed safely but after landing the wheel on the port side collapsed and we gently slewed over onto the left-wing. I assisted the passengers off the aircraft, and they were wonderful, remaining calm throughout the procedure. Then we waited for a bus which arrived not long after and we all settled in for the two-and-a-half-hour drive to Cairns where we arrived after dark. We found out later that the hydraulics had failed after take-off from Townsville.

Next day I flew supernumerary on Viscount Flight 461 Cairns/Townsville/Brisbane. All in a day's work. These are my memories of an incident 61 years ago.

LEONIE PLUMMER (JAMES)
Ex TAA Air Hostess (1956-1959)

INNISFAIL EMERGENCY LANDING VH-AEQ

Leonie Plummer in uniform 1956 - 1959

CHAPTER 11

Not A Hostess On This Flight

In the late 1950's I was a very junior DC-3 First Officer based in Sydney. One morning while I was on reserve, I had a call from TAA rostering telling me to get out to the airport to crew a flight from Sydney to Melbourne. Since I lived at Mosman, I had to hurry to get there for the 1000 hours (10.00 am) departure.

When I arrived, I discovered that I was crewing a freighter with Laurie Mackay as the Captain. As I walked out to the aircraft, I found out that our load was one racehorse. This was interesting, and I wondered how horses liked flying. Very rapidly, I found that this horse positively hated the whole idea. There was a ramp both sides and the horse had to walk up this and then turn left to get to his stall which had already been prepared by the ground engineers. Sounds simple but the horse did everything it could to avoid travelling "The Friendly Way". Finally, the horse was loaded and pushed into a padded stall towards the front of the aircraft.

COME FLY WITH ME ... ON A DC-3

We had no hostess, instead a strapper who was to look after the horse and keep him calm for the three-hour flight to Essendon. Captain Mackay discussed the flight with the strapper and explained that it would be smooth flying and that there should no problem keeping the horse quiet. Sounds great but it did not work out that way. The Captain explained to me that on flights carrying livestock, we always carried a gun in case the animal broke free. "But," he said, "this never happens".

Once we took off and climbed to our cruising height, Laurie suggested to me, "Go back, Rob, and see that all is well." This I did, and while the horse did not look happy, it appeared quiet and well-secured. So, I found the catering which had been put on board and poured a cup of tea for the horse-handler and then took same back to the cockpit for Laurie and myself. We both said, "Hurray, this is all going well".

We spoke too soon! Suddenly there were loud bangs coming from the cabin. "You better talk to the strapper and get him to keep that horse quiet," Laurie told me. The horse had discovered that he could kick the side of the fuselage and that was certainly not doing any good to our shiny DC-3. The strapper agreed, "Yes, I will try and secure him tighter so that he can't kick," and peace reigned for a few minutes!

When the banging and thumping started again, Laurie instructed me, "take that shotgun and go down and explain to the strapper that if the horse does not stop kicking our aeroplane to pieces, we will have to shoot him." The strapper turned pale and told me that the horse was racing in Melbourne that afternoon and he was worth many thousands of pounds! Anyway, we managed to rope him tighter and calm him down. Amazing what the threat of a gun can do – I don't think I could have brought myself to shoot him anyway.

This story did not end well as there was an accident unloading the horse. The ramp was not pulled closely enough to the fuselage, and as the horse plunged backwards, one of its legs slipped and tore a great deal of skin. Fortunately, no bones were broken, but we heard that the

NOT A HOSTESS ON THIS FLIGHT

horse did not race again for many weeks. I'll bet that when the horse returned to Sydney, it travelled by horse float!

DC-3's remained in service in considerable numbers well into the 1970s and I, personally, was still flying a DC-3 around Australia in 1990. Nearly everyone who has had anything to do with them has a sneaking affection for these aircraft in spite of the lack of pressurisation, very doubtful cabin heating and a noisy cabin. It also gave passengers a good view of the countryside as it rarely flew above 9,000 feet and cruised along at 150 knots or 300kms per hour. A far cry from today where you are 35,000 feet up and travelling at nearly the speed of sound.

ROB FRASER
Ex TAA Captain

CHAPTER 12

The Chunderbus

From Western Australia, Glenis Thompson sends contributions of DC-3 stories that she feels sure will interest other "early DC-3 girls".

The common name for the DC-3 when I was flying was The Chunderbus! I saw more people reach for the paper bag on the DC-3 than on any other aircraft. The flights were often bumpy and that, together with the bags of spuds, onions, an occasional dog etc., mixed with the galley smells did not help.

One young lad, a passenger, had consumed a pink milkshake before boarding and you can guess where that ended up – not in the sick bag! I think it was the same lad whose bladder did not cope because he was scared of the turbulence and then when we landed, he discovered that his beloved dog had not been loaded. I felt so sorry for him.

When we called at properties, the station wives were there to meet us. They had mail and other assorted items to post, and they loved a chat with another female. We were allowed to discard our pantyhose on western flights – often on just a station strip from which sheep had been buzzed prior to landing. The Captain or First Officer's first words were, "okay girls, off with your pantyhose!" Quite a relief as you can imagine. On one such flight, I was having a nap when the plane buzzed sheep on a station runway. I awoke with a start, heart hammering, I really thought we were going to crash.

On another DC-3 flight, the Pilot feathered an engine at Maroochydore, and we got a lift back to Brisbane on a freight plane.

I remember one flight we did was a "real" milk run. Brisbane, Roma, Mitchell, Charleville, Quilpie, Arrabury, Durham Downs, Nappa Merrie, Orientos and Tibooburra. I remember that there was a truck standing outside the pub – the biggest one I had ever seen.

25th – 29th January 1962, I crewed a DC-3 from Brisbane to Birdsville via Quilpie, Winton, Charleville, overnight Birdsville. I vaguely recall pulling our beds outside for the night where it was so much cooler. On to Adelaide for the next night and enjoyed a hot shower and "proper" toilet. Back to Birdsville and same sheets on the bed! Then to Brisbane via Thargomindah, Charleville. That would have been a five day Western so we must have overnighted in Charleville both ways.

Then, when I was transferred to Brisbane, my DC-3 days ended.

THE CHUNDERBUS

**Shower at Birdsville where the water was cold and brown.
I was scared of anything that may have been lurking there!**
Courtesy Glenis Thompson

COME FLY WITH ME … ON A DC-3

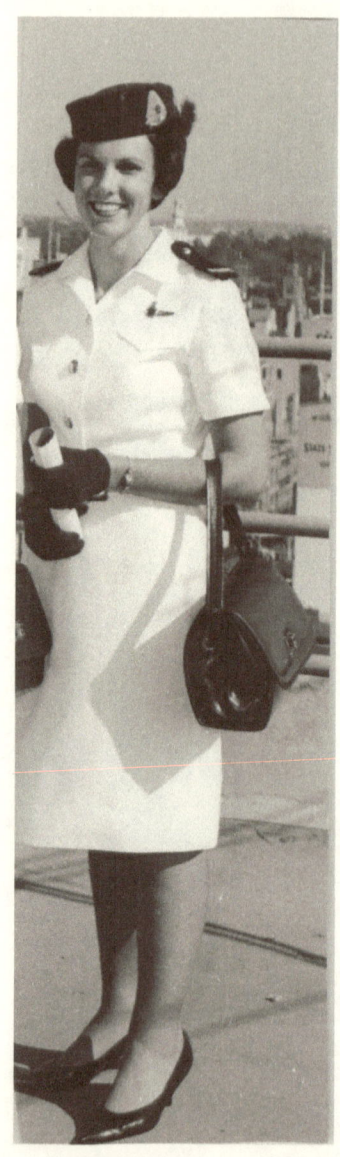

Glenis Thompson in uniform
Glenis Thompson (Playle)
Ex TAA Air Hostess (1961-1963)
Photo Glenis Thompson

CHAPTER 13

New Guinea DC-3 Adventures

An adventure I was part of, had been played out before somewhere in the United States of America when DC-3's were the main airline aircraft. My First Officer (whom we will call Leo) and I were carrying out a hospital charter (the Lae Hospital staff chartered an aircraft from TAA to take a group of people away for the weekend from Lae to Madang). We had one regular hostess, whom we will name Jill and another member, whom we will name Merv, who were our cabin attendants for the trip.

We knew that Merv was pretty keen on Jill, so if she asked him to do something he would not hesitate. When we had reached our cruising level, with the autopilot engaged, and were tracking up the Markham Valley, we called Jill up to the cockpit and told her to send Merv up when we rang the hostess call bell. We stacked all the baggage so that Leo could hide under the radio rack and I could secrete myself behind the bags in the forward baggage area. We placed our caps on our seats, opened each window and pressed the call button then dived into our hiding positions. Merv arrived, closing the cockpit door behind him and continued past us up to the front only to be confronted by the alarming scene we had arranged. He looked at the hats and the open windows and went back to the cockpit door and opened it, checking to see if we were down the back. Merv said that when he did not see us there, he thought that we had been sucked out and was preparing to take control and save the day! He had done a couple of hours flying training and was thinking just how he would handle the situation! Evidently, he thought that if Doris Day could do it in an old film then surely, he could do it. He was saved from having to do anything because we could no longer contain ourselves and were falling about with laughter so that the bags fell in on us, and our positions were revealed.

Flying at this time you must appreciate that we were operating piston engine, unpressurised, aircraft which were only able to maintain 5,000 to 7,000 feet on one engine, and because of the lack of pressurisation we had to descend at no more than 500 feet per minute so that passengers on board could equalise their ears to the increasing air pressure (termed "clear your ears"). Most of the river valleys were around 5,000 feet give or take a thousand. Naturally, the closer you got to the coast, the lower the valley floors were.

On one occasion, I got caught out by the bad weather that occurs every afternoon in the highlands. The trip was to proceed from Port Moresby to Mount Hagen and was scheduled to depart in the early afternoon. As usual, when dealing with Port Moresby, we were running late. This was of no great concern as it was a beautiful day with almost no build-ups over the hills. We headed along the southern side of the Owen Stanleys with the intention of flying up the valley of the Kaugel River to cover the last 20 miles to Mount Hagen. As we flew along in the bright, sunny day, I checked out the Asaro river valley which led to Goroka, and that was clear as far as the eye could see. This was an alternate route to Mount Hagen via the Asaro around Mount Michael (11,966 feet) then left past Mount Kerigomma (12,000 feet) over the ridge and into the Wahgi Valley and then west following the Wahgi to Mount Hagen.

The good weather continued so we carried on along the southern side of the Kubor range. As we reached the Kaugel, the cloud went down to ground level, so I thought "No worries, we'll go back and use the alternate route," which is what we did. When we turned up the Asaro Valley the cloud was starting to thicken ahead of us, so I called Goroka who advised that they had a thunderstorm overhead and the strip was closed. No worries, we would avoid the Goroka Valley and proceed as we intended into the Wahgi etc.

Listening out on the radio, we could hear traffic moving up and down the Wahgi, so it still looked okay. Wrong! As we passed Mount Michael the cloud went down to the ground ahead, so we turned around with the intention of returning to Port Moresby, but the cloud was closing in behind us – we were stuck! Mount Michael 11,966 feet on our right, Mount Kerigomma 12,000 feet on our left and the highest mountain, Mount Wilhelm 14,793 feet ahead and to our left. The only thing to do was put on our oxygen masks and climb up to 16,000 feet and head for Goroka radio station which kept us clear of any high rocks and then head for Madang.

Our instrument flying has never been so good! We caught all the updrafts and tried to avoid the downdrafts as we ploughed on through the storm over Goroka. We popped out of the cloud at 30 miles from Madang at 16,000 feet, and as we had to descend at around 500 feet per minute, it took some time to get down to sea level. Thirty-two minutes later, we arrived at Madang.

KERRY HUSTON
Ex TAA Captain

COME FLY WITH ME ... ON A DC-3

"Courage is the price that life extracts
for granting peace.
The soul that knows it not, knows no release...
From little things, knows not the livid loneliness of fear,
Nor mountain heights where bitter joy can hear...
The sound of wings."
Amelia Earhart

CHAPTER 14

A Hostess In Flight Mode

I vividly recall my first experience on a DC-3.

Based in Papua New Guinea (PNG) in 1972, I had mainly crewed the Fokker Friendship and enjoyed jaunts around the air in a Twin Otter. Nowhere on my current roster had I seen the need to familiarise myself with the interior of the DC-3.

Standby days in New Guinea were hard, as one had the choice of either lazing around on a floating bed in Lae's sunny pool, listening to Creedence Clearwater Revival on a tape recorder in one's donga, or taking a lazy walk in a mini Meri dress around the Mess chatting with other crew members.

This particular morning found me floating in the pool when I suddenly received notification that I was urgently required to crew a DC-3 to Wau. Wow!

COME FLY WITH ME ... ON A DC-3

Slipping quickly into my colourful uniform – this was the era of the liquorice all sorts uniform with choices of white, blue, pink or yellow, topped off with a navy and white striped deerstalker hat – I boarded the unfamiliar aircraft and busily set about coming to terms with this new challenge. The meals were all hooked into this big cannister contraption, and in fact, nothing much looked familiar. Flying in PNG was quite a different experience when compared with mainland flying, which was under strict training and regulations.

Following the Safety PA (in pidgin English), I pulled myself up the steep incline towards the cockpit to announce that the cabin was ready for take-off. I was almost there when the aircraft suddenly took off! There I was, hanging on for dear life, my arms flung ungracefully around the closest seat and my legs sliding downwards. There was little amusement on the faces of the indigenous passengers who just stared ahead or out the window at their families running alongside the strip wailing and with arms outstretched as the aircraft sped along the runway.

I guess they thought this was part of the norm. A hostess in flight mode!

No other aircraft offered such spectacular views as the DC-3, flying at only 8,000 feet above sea level. It was a sightseeing experience for all.

It wasn't until the DC-3 levelled, that I could restore my dignity and open the cockpit door. The surprise on the flight crew's face wasn't what I expected. "Why hello there, we didn't know we had a hostie today," was the greeting. "Welcome aboard."

To this day, I will never know if they were having a go at me or were seriously unaware.

Big smiles all round. This was New Guinea. Everything was okay.

As for the DC-3, I loved it from that moment on and still carry warm fuzzy memories of looking out the windows as I climbed my way up the

A HOSTESS IN FLIGHT MODE

aisle to the cockpit. Thereafter, I always waved energetically at the flight crew from the tarmac if I was suddenly called out while on standby.

Imagine this happening in today's airline world.

Barbara Hofmann
Ex TAA Air Hostess (1968-1973)

Barbara Hofmann

CHAPTER 15

TAA Memories

I joined TAA when the company commenced operations ex Brisbane. I worked for six years as a stenographer in the City Office and the Airport, finishing up as secretary for Captain Charles Gray, Senior Route Captain, Queensland. Then, in 1952, I was accepted as an Air Hostess, School 52 and trained in Melbourne where I stayed until February 1953 when I was posted to Brisbane.

During my flying time, I crewed DC-3's, DC-4's and the Convair and have many happy memories, particularly of the Queensland Outback.

According to my logbook (still in my possession), my first flight ex Brisbane was on a DC-3 to Townsville then changed to an L18 Lockheed Lodestar to Cairns where we spent an overnight at the TAA hostel, returning to Brisbane the following day. The flying time to Cairns was six hours and twenty-five minutes plus time spent on the ground checking.

DC-4's did not fly to Darwin ex Brisbane during my time with TAA. We flew on DC-3's taking approximately 12 hours or more flying time, landing at numerous towns on the way. The accommodation in Darwin was at Paspaley's Darwin Hotel, which was very upmarket compared to other towns. I do remember staying at the Queen's Hotel in Townsville, hotels in Longreach, Cloncurry and Tennant Creek and the TAA hostel in Cairns.

An incident that remains in my memory happened when I was serving meals and hit my knee on the seat adjustment lever which dislocated my knee, causing me to fling the tray up in the air, and I fell on a male passenger, leaving lipstick on his collar. As you can imagine, he was not too pleased, and I do not think he knew about the lipstick. I remember thinking, "I hope he is not married!"

I had more trouble with my knee on another flight, this time while being checked. The same thing happened again; however, no passengers were involved this time. After the pilot pulled my knee back into position, the check hostess took over for me. At least I was not checked that day!

On one of my first flights out west, an old Western character was passing around bottles of Scotch and handed one to the Captain for "the little girlie up the back".

While staying in Darwin on one trip, Mrs Paspaley invited some of us to view a crocodile "hunt" at night, which was exciting but also eerie.

The best thing about flying was people contact and the staff with whom I worked. I felt I grew up with TAA – it was like a big family in those days.

I had previously met my husband on a flight, and I resigned in 1954 as we were not allowed to work as a hostess when we married. We lived in Sydney then in Townsville for 22 years where a group of ex-hosties formed a Wings Away Branch, raising money for children's charities and enjoying social occasions.

ROMANCE IN THE AIR

While flying in Queensland, I crewed many Brisbane/Cairns flights, but this one stands out in my mind because it involved my future husband.

Neil was second mate on a merchant ship which happened to be berthed in Townsville on the way to Hong Kong for a six-month refit. When hearing that I would be overnight in Cairns, he booked on my flight as well as the return flight next morning. Crew members of a ship were not allowed to leave port, but with the assistance of his Chief Officer, he decided to go.

Next morning, we were worried that the ship might have already sailed, so descending into Townsville I went to the cockpit as we flew over the harbour to check that it was still berthed. It was – there followed a few anxious moments, but all was well.

And here is the punch line! Neil did not know that because there was a chance of a "wharfie" strike, the ship's Master had been told to sail immediately if the strike eventuated. Luckily for Neil, this did not happen.

Fleur Hanley (Bradbury)
Ex TAA Air Hostess (1952-1954)

Fleur Hanley, first day in uniform

CHAPTER 16

Qantas New Guinea Reminiscing

My first meeting with a DC-3, other than as a passenger on Butler's to Evans Head, was in 1954. I had completed a five-year apprenticeship as an Aircraft Maintenance Engineer with Qantas. Three years of this was at Rose Bay and the other two years at various overhaul sections at the Qantas Mascot Base. At the end of my apprentice training, having sat Department of Civil Aviation (DCA) basic and type examinations for a maintenance engineer license, I was sent to Qantas at Lae in the then Mandated Territory of New Guinea.

What a shock! I was detailed to "depart" and "arrive" a number of DC-3's – I had barely seen one before, but you soon learn the "deep end" training system. Check fuel and oil on board with dipstick and co-pilot then secure the caps. With crew in their seats, remove the undercarriage down lock pins and pitot cover, display to pilot, place in rear door stowage bag, door closed and callout to crew "Pins and pitots removed and stowed, hatches closed and locked, clear to start."

COME FLY WITH ME ... ON A DC-3

Engines were started, signal for chocks out given, and then done, thumbs up and away it goes.

We sometimes worked weekends, and as compensation for the no penalty rates system, we could have two days off mid-week in Lae, not the entertainment capital of Asia. Or, you could spend two days as an untrained and unpaid flight attendant. The up side was you got to see a bit of New Guinea, if only from the air, and basic grass aerodromes. One charter service I recall was called a most un-politically correct name, but the second word was "run". You can fill in the spaces. It was used to position indentured labour lines around the territory.

This operated from Lae on Thursdays. It went to Madang, Wewak's Borum strip, Lorengau naval base on Manus Island, Kavieng and Rabaul. Overnight was at Rabaul and a return to Lae the next morning. A few overwater sectors were involved, but I do not recall any life jackets or where you would stow them. The overnight at Rabaul was memorable for the volcanic dust everywhere and the ground that vibrated from the diesel power unit providing town power.

I did another trip from Lae to Port Moresby transporting some aged locals for medical treatment in the Capital. We flew high, above 10,000 feet, and it was cold. I looked back through the flight station door, and the old folk were shaking, and their teeth were chattering. So, I turned on the cabin heating system. This takes heat from each engine's exhaust through heat exchangers, and some cable operated valves and delivers a musty-smelling blast of warm air into the cabin. It never did work well or smoothly. I looked back on the passengers a few minutes later, and they were changing slowly to a greenish tinge. So, off with the cabin heat and let them freeze, it was the preferable path to go to avoid a clean-up at Moresby.

After about a year in Lae and with my Maintenance Engineer's license having been delivered in October, I applied for a relocation to the city of Port Moresby. This was granted as I had considerable experience with Catalina and Sandringham flying boats and could sign out

QANTAS NEW GUINEA REMINISCING

DC-3's operating out of Jacksons Aerodrome. I left Lae accompanied by my BSA motorcycle, unloaded it at Jacksons, pinched some petrol from the aircraft, since the bike had to be empty for the flight, and rode into town.

Some of the DC-3 operations out of Jacksons were charters for plantations. Bales of rubber out and food and household goods for the return. The rubber bales looked like giant erasers and the local cargo loaders delighted in kicking them out the cargo door where they would bounce around on the tarmac. If a magani (small wallaby) appeared they would take-off in pursuit, and any loading could wait.

Seating was 46 passengers, the original side facing "soap dish" seats from the military C47, a further side facing row made of steel tube and canvas facing the existing right-hand side seats and two double row tube steel and canvas seats forward-facing near the main door. Two pilots and two "cabin attendants".

Here is a typical transit stop with cargo and passengers deplaning together. Notice bag on cargo door for pins, pitot covers, and fuel dipsticks mentioned earlier.

COME FLY WITH ME ... ON A DC-3

QANTAS DC-3 in New Guinea, courtesy Frank Shipway

One of the interesting stops, for me, was Borum, the airstrip for Wewak. Embedded in the side of the strip were some parts of wrecked aircraft. The interesting one was a Japanese-made Daimler Benz DB 601, the engine from the Messerschmitt 109 and 110. They had been built under license from the Germans, but it had an American-designed Hamilton Standard propeller adapted to fit the German propeller shaft. The Japanese had a license from the United States (US) propeller maker and used their propeller designs in many of their aircraft during the war. I wonder if royalties were paid during or after the war? The small building in the background was the airport's public facilities. Clearly based on a western Queensland design.

At Moresby, I had my first contact with the Douglas DC-4. What a revelation, a relatively modern design with parts that fit together without great effort.

Here I am in 1955, same ears as now, more or less white overalls and safety shoe sandals with a DC-4 in the background.

Frank Shipway with a DC-4 New Guinea

COME FLY WITH ME ... ON A DC-3

Moresby 1955

I can mention here one of the minor disasters that occurred during a turnaround of a DC-4 at Jacksons. One of the cargo handlers was very keen to work for the engineering group, so he was given a trial. First job, after full instruction, was to empty the toilet tank. This was a large tank down toward the rear of the aircraft arranged to collect and store the contents of the dual toilets. It had a drain valve accessed through a panel that upon pulling of a cable lanyard would smartly open the valve, discharging the tank contents. However, before this could happen a rectangular funnel and large hose was attached with pins to the aircraft which was sealed around the edges so no spillage could occur. The hose was connected to a wheeled tank to carry off the aircraft tank contents.

The trainee attached the funnel and pulled the lanyard – nothing happened, so he removed the funnel, looked up at the valve while pulling the lanyard. Of course, in accordance with that Irishman's Law, it worked a treat! The spray spread over a fair area and coated some of the passenger's bags resting in an adjacent luggage trolley. The trainee lost any enthusiasm for working for Engineering, and his friends laughingly said in tok pisin "he wash wash in pec pec". You can make your own translation.

The DC-4 would fly nonstop from Brisbane and arrive just on dawn. Engineering had the task of ascertaining the ETA (Expected Time of Arrival) from Jackson's control tower and then advise others involved. So, the deal was, early morning you rang Moresby exchange with a hand-cranked magneto phone and asked to be switched to Jackson's tower. That was the intended system. After the third try, you would get out the motorbike, ride the few miles into the exchange, awaken the operator and then talk to the tower.

We had a fair number of local staff that were housed in a large shed-like building in the valley behind the mess. They would need awakening. I will never forget, when the door was opened, the eye-watering smell of sweat and twist tobacco smoked as "roll your owns" using the Sydney Morning Herald as cigarette paper.

Frank Shipway
Airworthiness Inspector and Consultant

CHAPTER 17

Memories Of Ansett-ANA Days

It was Christmas Day, 1964, and I had been rostered to crew a DC-3 to Deniliquin, Hay and Griffith in New South Wales then back to Melbourne on an Ansett-ANA Air Coach Service.

It was an extremely hot day which made the flying rough and bumpy.

We did not serve meals in those days, only water, and the aircraft is almost fully loaded with passengers who are not happy with the turbulence we are experiencing. My constant job was walking up the aisle to collect the sick bags, using one myself, then back to collect more full ones from the passengers. I was never so relieved as when we arrived at our destination, Griffith.

Since it was Christmas Day, the Airport Manager gave the two pilots and myself a small Christmas fruitcake each, which was a pleasant surprise. It was just as rough on the return trip to Melbourne, but fortunately, we did not have many passengers. The pilots ate their cake for afternoon tea, but I saved mine and enjoyed it when I reached home.

During the football season in 1964, I was rostered on an Ansett-ANA Air Coach Service to Sale, a town in the Eastern part of Victoria. It was a particularly cloudy day, and as we were getting closer to our destination, the cloud became denser. We had a plane full of football fans who were pretty happy as their team had won, so they were not unduly concerned about the weather as the cloud closed in.

In those days radar was non-existent in that area, and the DC-3 was not pressurised so we could not fly over ten thousand feet to get above the thick cloud. The Captain asked me to find someone on board who knew the area well.

I will never forget it as I brought the gentleman into the cockpit, and he was asked to stand behind the Captain. We could just see the river through the cloud hanging around us, and this football fan (I think he owned the hotel) directed the Captain as he followed the river with its twists and bends to our destination. Finally, we arrived safe and sound at Sale.

Annie Butt (MacDonald)
Ex Ansett-ANA Air Hostess (1963-1968)

CHAPTER 18

Taxi!

On the day of my arrival at Eagle Farm Airport, Brisbane, after travelling supernumerary from Melbourne, I experienced my first adventure although not in the air as you might expect but on the ground!

TAA found accommodation for me in a one-room unit in Roma Street and after reading the extensive list of rules tacked on the back of the door; I decided it was not for me.

Here I was in a strange city in a complete quandary. My knowledge of Brisbane was negligible so, still dressed in my white uniform, I went out and bought a newspaper and searched for alternative digs. Eventually, I found a place in New Farm, and after asking the girl at the desk about how to get there, I set off.

I decided to walk across the Storey Bridge, not knowing how long it was. It seemed to stretch forever into the distance, so while I walked, I tried to hail a taxi. At last, one pulled up beside me, and I climbed in grateful for the ride. The driver knew the address, so when we arrived, I asked him to wait while I inspected the flat.

COME FLY WITH ME ... ON A DC-3

He nodded and said, "Sure, I can wait for you, take your time."

Ten minutes later I returned to the taxi. "Can you take me back to Roma Street?" I asked the patient driver.

When we arrived at the complex, I enquired, expecting to pay a huge fare, "How much do I owe you?"

"Oh," he said with a cheeky grin, "I'm not a taxi but happy to help out."

An anecdote from Fay:

> "I was rostered to crew a 'Brisbane Lights at Night' flight for the Coronation. After we had been airborne for some time, one of the passengers buzzed and asked, "Are they stars we are passing?" I had to disillusion her by telling her, "No, they are not stars; they are sparks from the exhaust!"

Fay Lambert (Goodger)
Ex TAA Air Hostess (1952-1954)

CHAPTER 19

Not Always A Bed Of Roses!

The only Queensland western flight that was on the bottom of my favourite list, was the Brisbane-Tennant Creek overnight. It was a long flight departing at first light arriving in Tennant Creek around 1630 (4.30pm) South Australian time. Unfortunately, the day's heat still hung in the air and stepping out of the aircraft's cabin was like stepping into an oven.

Dinner was the usual fare, limp lettuce leaf, beetroot, tomato, cucumber, onion and cold corned beef while dessert was usually custard and tinned fruit, but it was adequate, and the servings were generous. At night sleep was near impossible until midnight, when a cool breeze wafted in from the desert, and the bedsheets cooled down, for we slept in an upstairs netted verandah that was open to the weather – no air conditioning, no fans, in fact there was no air conditioning anywhere in Queensland when I was flying, sometimes fans.

COME FLY WITH ME ... ON A DC-3

I was on standby duty one evening and on checking the roster found that one of the early morning flights was the Brisbane-Tennant Creek overnight. The hostess rostered was well known for pulling out in the early hours of the morning citing ear trouble. My housemates warned me and suggested I prepare for the flight before bed. I was tired and did not heed their advice, and so I paid the price!

At 0300 (3.00am) the shrill peal of the telephone awakened all of us – I was to work the Tennant Creek flight, pick-up 0400 (4.00am). That did not leave me much time to prepare, so everyone crawled out of bed to help. While I bathed and packed an overnight bag, Fay ironed my uniform, Mavis polished my buttons, buckle, and half wings (they had a habit of becoming tarnished very quickly) and Del cleaned my shoes and made me coffee and toast. Luckily for me, they were all at home, and not a word of complaint passed their lips. All I had to do was step into my uniform and put on my face. I was ready on time but not a great start to a long day.

My housemates fell into bed to catch up on some sleep, and when I was next rostered on standby duty, I was fully prepared for every flight. Yes, I had learned another lesson – the hard way!

At the end of a long day that stretches into night and as the DC-3 heads towards Eagle Farm Airport enveloped in darkness, the twinkling lights of Brisbane are a welcome sight.

Flying out west at night is spectacular, the occasional lights of an isolated town or station property break the inky blackness around us or sometimes a ring of fire like a horseshoe comes into view, the fractured orange circle burning unchecked and I always hope that it does not encroach on properties or towns making it dangerous for both people and animals.

Night landing is fascinating. It is a time when the city is at its best with sparkling lights of all shapes and sizes, arterial roads are easily discernible by the steady stream of traffic, and all of this comes together to give the city a blueprint of life after dark.

Sometimes the navigational lights of another aircraft appear in the distance or the warning lights attached to tall structures, to prevent collisions, catch my eye. At night, lights define a city, and as we circle and approach the runway, I turn off the cabin lights. The wheels drop and lock, and the aircraft's landing lights flood the runway. As we descend, the city's lights grow larger and my day is almost over. The aircraft touches down, there is a slight skid of wheels, and we race along the runway. When we finally slow down, we turn and taxi to the TAA Airport Lounge. I help the passengers with their luggage from the overhead racks and bid them goodnight then I start the checking before heading home myself. My day will soon be over, and I will leave Eagle Farm with the memory of a night sky firmly entrenched in my mind, a night sky that truly sparkles.

Being an Air Hostess was not always a bed of roses. It meant that we had to be continually conscious of our behaviour and our dress presentation.

While working in Sydney, I was rostered on a direct Sydney/Adelaide flight, and we had on board, travelling as a passenger, a Check Hostess from Melbourne. I was wearing my white summer uniform and navy suit coat as it was cold when we left, and this was acceptable as a form of dress. Unfortunately for me, the other hosties were wearing winter uniform, navy skirt and suit coat with a white blouse that sported a rounded Peter Pan collar over the coat's neckline.

When we were checking catering for the return flight after the Adelaide passengers had disembarked, I received a message asking me to report to the Adelaide Supervisor's office. When I arrived, I was greeted by the Melbourne Check Hostess. "What are you doing in summer uniform? You look like Black and White Scotch Whisky! You should be wearing winter uniform," she reprimanded.

"I don't have a winter uniform. I am on loan to Sydney from Brisbane," I explained, mortified to be ticked off, at the age of 23, in front of several Adelaide hosties. "We don't wear winter uniform in Queensland," I added.

"In that case, as soon as you land back in Brisbane make arrangements to fly to Melbourne for a skirt fitting. That's all!" and I was dismissed! I walked back to the aircraft suitably chastised, and when I returned to Brisbane, I approached my port Supervisor. She was not happy either. "I don't have enough girls to let you go," she complained sighing heavily. "I suppose I don't have an option. Down one day, back the next mind you."

That day preparations were made for me to travel supernumerary to Melbourne and I was duly fitted for a skirt which I made sure I wore during winter months when flying south of the border. Black and White Scotch Whisky? I appreciate the analogy!

NOT ALWAYS A BED OF ROSES!

Sometimes we carried passengers who were too ill to sit in a seat, so they travelled by stretcher. Seats were removed and the stretcher slotted into the floor. One young boy I had on board a couple of times, was a bright, polite child. His mother and father travelled with him and sat in the double seats behind his head so that they could monitor his condition throughout the flight.

I always made sure he was well wrapped up in rugs as it could be cold on the floor of a DC-3, but he never complained. At mealtimes (he was travelling to Brisbane for medical treatment) I would cut up his food so that he could eat easily with a fork. I often thought about him and hoped his treatment had helped.

On another occasion, a Brisbane/Townsville flight, we collected a baby travelling alone from Rockhampton to Townsville. A second hostess, Sylvia, had been delegated as his carer for the flight. I will never forget how ill and undernourished he looked and so tiny for his age. Poor child had severe diarrhoea, and we were held up at each landing while we changed him. After taking off from Proserpine I noticed his lips were blue which meant lack of oxygen, so I reported to the Captain who requested permission to fly low into Townsville Airport. This was granted, and he also requested an ambulance to meet the aircraft when we landed.

When the baby's mother realised that the ambulance was for her child, she burst into tears as she told us he was a healthy baby when he left for Rockhampton. That night we all worried about him, concerned for his well-being and on the way to the airport next morning, the Captain called into the hospital to check on his progress. He was doing fine after a night of care, so we headed out to the airport happy that the baby's condition had rapidly improved.

COME FLY WITH ME … ON A DC-3

On an overnight western in Charleville, I was approached after dinner by a guy I had met through friends on a couple of social occasions in Townsville.

After chatting for a few minutes, he said to me, "Joy, why don't you drive back to Brisbane with me tomorrow?"

I looked at him in disbelief. "No! Definitely No! I am on duty and crew the early morning flight back to Brisbane tomorrow."

"But," he insisted, "you have another hostess on the flight, she could work for you."

"Good heavens!" I exclaimed, horrified at the suggestion, "The other hostess is my Port Supervisor, and she is returning on the direct flight to Brisbane."

Next day there was a note in my mailbox requesting I report to the Supervisor, which I did without delay. I was faced with an angry Supervisor who immediately sought to clarify the situation. "Your friend out at Charleville asked me to accompany him back to Brisbane in his car. He said you had to work," she paused, glaring at me, "Did you suggest that he approach me?"

"I most certainly did not," I assured her, angry myself now that this guy could be so audacious and put me in such a difficult position. I never saw him again, which was just as well because I would have been icily polite and scathing about his behaviour.

NOT ALWAYS A BED OF ROSES!

There were always passengers who made you feel good about being an Air Hostess. On one flight from Sydney to Brisbane, I had as passengers, the talented and famous pianist, Winifred Atwell, who was born in Trinidad, and her husband. She was a friendly person, and after chatting for a few moments about her career, she told me she had studied as a classical pianist at the Royal Academy of Music, London. I asked her, "How do you practice when you are staying in hotels? Hours of piano playing would create a noise problem for some people surely?"

She laughed and said, "Good question. I carry with me a silent keyboard, so I can play for as long as I like without worrying other guests." What a wonderful idea! However, I would not have minded being in the room next door!

At one of our recent Wings Away luncheons held at *INBOUND*, in the Toowoomba Railway Station, our member, Beres Hindman (McLennan) brought along a friend, Thelma, who told me that when she, her husband and ten-year-old son were flying home to Queensland, the Air Hostess asked them if they would like tea or coffee and after taking their order she moved on to their son. "What would you like to drink young man?" she queried, and without hesitation, he replied, "Tea, please."

"Would you like black or white tea?" the Hostess asked. The young boy thought for a couple of seconds then being a bush kid, he answered seriously, "Brown, please." A good one!

It is interesting to note here that INBOUND is owned by Meredith and her husband, Mark, and we usually meet there every month for lunch. Meredith's mother, Nerolie Shean, was a TAA hostie based in Sydney and her father, Jeffery Bennett, was a TAA Captain. We are always well looked after by the friendly staff; sometimes by her daughter, Emma and son Alex (an Astrophysicist studying his Masters in Finland), besides which the food is tasty and beautifully presented and in the winter months, we can sit near a roaring log fire. Great ambience for a social get-together!

NOT ALWAYS A BED OF ROSES!

Ex Hosties Toowoomba Christmas 2018

Standing:
Sue Carey (TAA) Annie Butt (Ansett ANA) Cathy Haynes (QANTAS) Judy Potts (QANTAS)
Seated: Mary McCurran (TAA) Joy Allardyce (TAA) Laurel Fraser (TAA) Pat Ashman (Ansett)

I was never too happy about having football teams on board. They enjoyed a drink, or two, or three then they would end up moving around the cabin talking and laughing uproariously whereupon the Captain would request that they all remain seated which suited me fine. The worst team I had on a flight from Brisbane to Longreach was an American team of lively young men. I breathed a sigh of relief when we arrived at our destination, and we said goodbye. I was exhausted – I ran miles that day!

However, I could not believe my luck when I realised, I had been rostered to bring them back to Brisbane after the games. They were a quieter group on the return trip, and there were a few bandaged arms in slings, some players limping and some with facial bruises. Despite this, they still managed to demand endless attention. Their Manager spent part of the trip with me in the tail, and we both lamented about their behaviour.

One good thing about carrying passengers who drank too much and became a nuisance was that we could close the bar; no more alcoholic drinks would be served. We had the authority to do this, but of course it was not a popular decision with some passengers, nevertheless a necessary one, particularly for those passengers who were not part of the offending group.

After the Korean War Truce Agreement had been signed in August 1953, some of the Royal Australian Air Force (RAAF) pilots who had been based in Japan were posted to Archerfield. (They had a humorous nickname for the capital of North Korea Pyongyang. It was "ping pong"). I spent many happy hours in their company; they were good fun. We went fishing, swimming, on picnics, day trips to Surfers Paradise which was mainly sand dunes along the beachfront and holiday houses across the road, just a hop, step and a jump from a swim in the ocean and fish and chips at the end of the day. One of the RAAF wives, Pat, with whom I became friendly, was an ex Qantas hostie and when I was offered two kittens by the agents at Roma, she said she would have one. Unfortunately, I was on an overnight when they arrived at the city TAA office so Pat said she would pick them up. When they opened the box containing the cats, two spitting bullets leapt into the air and ran up the curtains while pandemonium ensued. An hour later the cats were rounded up and placed back into the box for the ride to Pat's home. I don't think I was too popular for a couple of days!

NOT ALWAYS A BED OF ROSES!

I attended many parties at the Archerfield Officers Mess, but one night we were invited to a gathering at Amberley Air Base. It was a great night, but unfortunately, the car broke down on the way home, and we were stranded. A calamity for me as I had an early morning pick-up and the thought of a long flight ahead without much sleep was not the best of situations. Worse than that was knowing what would happen if I did not appear when the pick-up car arrived!

There we were, in the middle of the road, (no mobile telephone in those days), no passing traffic we could wave down and precious time slipping away. Shirley Bostock (Hyland) (deceased), also an Air Hostess with TAA was a great comfort and positive that all would be well. It was. At last, a car came into view, its headlights highlighting the four of us standing beside the car, and the driver stopped and asked if he could help. Before driving off, he promised to contact someone to fix our problem. To cut a long story short, I did arrive home in time to change and greet the pick-up car as though nothing untoward had happened. A great relief after an anxious couple of hours! One of my housemates who had a couple of days off told me she was prepared to cover for me and take my place if I had been delayed. How fantastic! Next day, after the long flight to Cairns, I was relieved to reach the hostel for some relaxation, a shower and a good night's sleep before the return trip the next day.

Reminds me of a friend Jan Brennan British Airways, (deceased) who was still asleep when a frantic phone call awakened her. The crew was already at the New York airport, and the flight to England was close to leaving. Jan arrived in civilian clothes and changed into uniform in the aircraft while it was taxiing out to the runway for take-off! Oh, the joy of being an Air Hostess!

COME FLY WITH ME ... ON A DC-3

The Christmas festive season was always hectic in TAA. I worked every Christmas day and when I transferred to Melbourne Port at the end of 1954, I crewed three Convair direct flights from Melbourne to Hobart and each trip was fully loaded. On that day we carried 240 passengers just on that one route. I know it hardly compares with today's air traffic movements, but in the early 1950's when air travel was comparatively new, it was certainly seen as heavy loading. The big plus was that people were able to visit families and friends for a few days without having to spend half their holiday time travelling.

While based in Brisbane I was sometimes rostered to crew an East West Airlines DC3 return flight to Tamworth. I enjoyed the different scenery and the cabin arrangement was similar so the aircraft was easy to work.

On one occasion, TAA was requested to provide air hostesses to act as usherettes at a charity film showing at a city cinema. It was a film to do with flying and, although I am unable to recall its name, I do remember it was a war film about pilots and flying during the second world war.

We met in the foyer, wearing full summer white uniform (there were eight of us) to be briefed on seat configuration. Faye Lambert (Goodger), Iris Brown (Bauer) and myself were delegated to the dress circle, so we ran upstairs for a quick look at the rows of seats – where did the seat numbers start, where did they end, how did the rows run, A B C etc.? We had heaps of fun, especially in the dark once the lights had dimmed. The film buffs were very patient with our amateur efforts not realising that we were more at home in the air rather than on the ground and, in those days, usherettes did wear special uniforms so they would not have paid too much attention until our photograph appeared in the newspaper next day. We hoped the charity made lots of money and we were very happy to help them, it was certainly something different!

"Usherettes" at Charity Film

From Back to Front: Iris Brown (Bauer), Del Pellow (Wilesmith), Joy Allardyce (Shipway), Faye Lambert (Goodger), Irene Davis, Shirley Foster (Kennedy)

Left to Right: Inez Laycock, Mary Ellis (Quinn)

After I resigned from TAA I lost touch with some of my friends and for many years I tried to find Bridie O'Connor but to no avail. I wrote to Wings Away, Melbourne, requesting information from the members, unfortunately no one knew of her whereabouts. Then, sometime later, in the Sydney newsletter AIRLINES there appeared an appeal for any members who knew Bridie and I immediately contacted Flora Devery (Christian) who had inserted the request and my journey began.

COME FLY WITH ME ... ON A DC-3

It ensued that her eldest son, Brian, a resident of Norfolk Island (where I once lived) was searching for friends of his mother, anyone who had known her while she was an air hostess. I was elated when Flora gave me Brian's contact number but my happy thoughts were shattered when he told me that his mother had passed away in 1999. I felt a great sadness that Bridie and I were not able to catch up but great joy that I was speaking to her son, as Bridie had telephoned me when Brian was born.

Now Brian and his lovely wife Carol are good friends of mine and often visit me when they come to Australia to stay with their son who lives on the Gold Coast. I have also met his beautiful daughter, Sophie (who reminds me of Bridie) and her son Ollie and I know deep down that Bridie would be delighted about our friendship.

This bond would never have been possible without our wonderful network within Wings Away. My thanks to Flora and to Wings Away for making this possible.

NOT ALWAYS A BED OF ROSES!

Bridie O'Connor

CHAPTER 20

Townsville Duty

While working out of Brisbane port, we were also required to do six-week stints based in Townsville. TAA had a flat, not far from the beach, behind the Seaview Hotel. It was a dreary affair, full of cane furniture, worn carpets, cracked linoleum and dark corners that hosted innumerable spiders and their webs. On my first night, sleep was sporadic for it was stifling under the mosquito net, but at least the dive-bombing mosquitoes were thwarted in their mission. The nets were also a boon for preventing spiders from becoming bed mates. I often awakened in the morning only to find a hairy huntsman spider clinging to the net watching me with beady little eyes. I was grateful for the net!

A study of the Townsville hostess roster showed an endless list of Mount Isa (The Isa) overnights. The mining town seemed so far away, in the middle of nowhere.

On my first morning, the pick-up car tooted and after a short drive, we arrived at the terminal lounge. It was crammed with people, some of whom mopped at shiny red faces, jostling each other for a position

COME FLY WITH ME ... ON A DC-3

under the solitary fan. There were three flights scheduled to leave; one north, one south and one west. The Lockheed Lodestar from Cairns had just taxied in and unloaded its passengers and the DC-3 for the Townsville/Brisbane flight was having a clean-up in preparation. The Hostess from Cairns looked smart in white; I was the odd one out since western flights called for grey uniforms – less likely to show the dirt! The flight crew working the Townsville/Brisbane flight had stayed overnight at the elegant Queen's Hotel, which I think later became home of the Australian Broadcasting Commission (ABC).

So, my friends, come fly with me to The Isa, enjoy the thrill of flying low between ports and there are quite a few. Charters Towers, Richmond, Hughenden, Julia Creek, Cloncurry with an overnight in The Isa.

First chore, as always, sign the flight crew book, walk out to the aircraft and commence checking half an hour before take-off. You would be right in thinking that checking is a repetitive bore, but it is an essential chore for each flight is different – different route, different ports of call, could be scheduled for morning or afternoon and of course, different passengers. However, some travellers often fly the same route so there were some familiar faces and that is what I enjoyed most of all, meeting the passengers and being able to help them if needed.

By the time we are ready for boarding, my make-up has melted, and the back of my uniform clutches at my skin like a wet suit. I look forward to being airborne and the fresh air rushing through the air vents.

The flight is uneventful, apart from all the landings and take-offs, not many passengers, a couple of commercial travellers with a sprinkling of station workers and Mt Isa Mines staff. The pilots track along the railway line flying low between ports of call, no flight radar in 1953. As I watch the ground below appear and disappear, I see a red kangaroo standing in the slim shade of a telegraph pole. What a unique photograph that would make and I feel sorry for the kangaroo as the land is sparsely vegetated.

TOWNSVILLE DUTY

We arrive in The Isa late afternoon, landing on the runway that was used as the gliding strip when I lived there in the 1970s. There is a haze hanging over the town from the mine's stack, and it is hot, a dry heat, one that sears the nostrils. The agent drives us into the town to the Mt Isa Hotel, and before dinner, I take a stroll around the town. Just as I reach the hotel on my way back, one of the swinging doors to the bar bursts open and two men tumble out fist fighting. One, a lanky young drover, by the look of his boots, jeans and battered Akubra, sees me and for a split second he halts, raises his hat and out of the corner of his mouth says, "Excuse me," and promptly continues fighting, leaving me speechless on the pavement, overcome by the beery smell emanating from the hotel bar and marvelling at the young man's courtesy while physically otherwise engaged.

After dinner, I sit talking to the manager's wife while the pilots enjoy a beer with the manager, who is ex RAAF. A big surprise when I learn that we had both attended the same school at Maroubra, a Sydney suburb. Maroubra Beach has since been named "one of the most beautiful beaches in the world." We spoke of Sydney in hushed voices, the way people do when they meet, talk and reminisce many miles away from home.

That night I did not foresee that I would spend five years in The Isa during the 1970s while my husband worked as a senior doctor with the Royal Flying Doctor Service (RFDS).

We had a small group of ex-hosties in The Isa, Olga Bosso (TAA), Trish Fenton (Ansett), Thelma Hughes (TAA), and Lorraine McDonald (TAA) and we met monthly for lunch and a few laughs about flying days. The TAA girls, including me, belonged to Wings Away, the ex-hostie Association and in those days TAA gave us free air travel, First Class with champagne and meals, to attend the Brisbane Wings Away annual reunion dinner. I am still a member, although not an active one and was editor of AIRLINES, our newsletter, for a few years, together with the help of Laurel Fraser and her husband, Rob. Queensland is the only state still involved with fundraising as the other states have ceased functioning and have become friendship clubs.

I have digressed—back to the flight. The Mt Isa Hotel was a timber, two-storey building and at night when the heat of the day abated there were lots of creepy noises, creaks, squeaks and thuds. I was known to put a chair against the door as there was an endless stream of footsteps in the corridor, doors opening, doors closing, shouting in the street below and when all the noise died down, and people slept a quietness descended and every eerie sound was magnified.

Next morning, after a restless night, at 0630 (6.30am) when we departed from The Isa, the air was faintly warm, and an orange glow crept over the hills, the promise of another day loaded with heat.

During winter months, standing on the Mt Isa strip waiting for loading to be completed, teeth chattering, feet stamping to combat the cold creeping up from the ground, I found my grey uniform plus winter suit coat to be insufficient protection against the bitterly cold wind blowing in from the desert. While living in The Isa in the 1970s, the water in the horse trough iced over at night so there were two climatic extremes – summer days over 40 degrees and winter nights often below zero. Life must have been difficult when the mine began, and The Isa was primarily a tent town.

The breakfast hop between Mt Isa and Cloncurry, flying in a DC-3, was a real test of endurance. With a full aircraft, as it usually was, it meant serving 21 passengers plus two flight crew in 25 minutes flying time. When I was a novice to Outback flying, I took the safe way out and served Cloncurry passengers first, but it soon became an obsession that every passenger on board be served, even though some were still eating when we landed! I crouched like a sprinter on take-off, and as soon as possible, I would be off.

One of the main problems was chasing sausages swimming in gravy around the containers that were one on top of the other in the steel urns strapped to the floor. These urns had to be lifted from floor to buffet, and my hips continually bore bruises from being flung around the buffet while being challenged by the tail's unpredictable behaviour.

TOWNSVILLE DUTY

Chasing sausages in gravy was a frustrating chore, that is where tongs came in handy, although the sausages tended to slide away and disappear so, in the end, it was sheer determination that they eventually met their fate – on a passenger's plate!

I only did two Townsville assignments, one during 'the dry' and the other during cyclone season. I enjoyed my time in Townsville mainly because I was able to get to know other hosties who were rostered with me and because I made friends with itinerant people within the community. I swam in a protected ocean pool not far from the flat on days off and at the end of each posting returned to Brisbane as brown as a berry. Then there was beautiful Magnetic Island, reached by ferry and trips up into the mountains where I swam in the icy waters of a pool, so refreshing on a hot day, and the occasional dinner with friends at The Queen's Hotel. I also remember walking in the rain in a plastic raincoat and being just as wet inside the coat as I was on the outside, plastic incited perspiration and the steamy heat during the wet season was relentless.

During the Townsville stint, we sometimes crewed an aircraft back to Brisbane and stayed overnight. Since I was based in Brisbane, I would go home for the night, but one day when I checked my box for letters, there was a note from Mavis telling me we had moved house and she had packed all of my possessions, and we were now residing at a new address. I took a taxi to the new address and was astonished to find two Sydney girls, one of whom was a friend Patsy Booth (Sedgwick) (deceased) and another whom I had not met. They had been transferred for a couple of weeks to work out of Brisbane port. It was great catching up on all the news of my Sydney friends, but I was off again the next day and did not see them again while they were there. After a short posting was over, I was always glad to return to base, especially during 'the wet'.

COME FLY WITH ME ... ON A DC-3

Photograph of main street in Mount Isa,
courtesy of Rob Fraser

Photo of TAA Mount Isa Advertisement

CHAPTER 21

Tyre Blowout

On a western return flight to Brisbane, we blew a tyre on landing at Winton. This meant that we were forced to wait for hours while a replacement DC-3 plus tyre was found and stand-by pilots, as well as an engineer, alerted.

It was January, and the fierce sun beat down like a hammer. I felt like a wilting flower by the time we reached the local café, but at least we were in the shade as we sat in a cubicle drinking coffee, eating sandwiches and having a bit of a moan about the long delay. It was hot and airless, and we were just beginning to wonder whether we would see the lights of Brisbane or have to stay overnight when the agent raced in, "Good news," he called out from the doorway, "Your replacement should be here in half an hour." A sigh of relief that we would soon be on our way and we ordered a final cup of coffee to celebrate, hoping that Brisbane did not forget to load catering for the return flight for we still had two more ports of call before the final leg.

A taxi collected us while the agent picked up the two passengers and luggage from his office then we headed out to the strip. Since all the windows were down in the taxi, we were blasted by a dry, hot wind that could be called natural air conditioning, if you had a sense of humour!

So, there we were standing on the edge of the strip ecstatic that we would soon be airborne as the DC-3 circled and approached to land. A welcome sight! We could not believe what we saw next, the aircraft was coming in to land on one engine. "Oh, no!" we exclaimed in one voice as the DC-3 touched down, making a perfect landing despite the loss of an engine.

When the aircraft taxied in, and the pilots and an engineer emerged, our hopes were dashed by their serious facial expressions, however, before long they were unable to contain their mirth at our disappointment and with wide grins told us that the Captain had feathered the engine as a practical joke. We were slightly mollified but not impressed after our long sojourn in the heat and felt no sympathy for the relieving crew as we climbed into the aircraft, loaded the passengers and luggage and waved goodbye, leaving them in the unrelenting heat while the engineer changed the tyre.

Winton also played a part in a surreal overnight for me. The hotel had curtains on the bedroom doorways, hardly a deterrent for unwanted visitors. My first challenge was when I went to the bathroom to shower and found hundreds of huge brown grasshoppers clinging to walls, the floor and anywhere they could gain a grip. Needless to say, I backed out hoping they would have taken wing by early morning.

The next challenge came not long after I had fallen asleep when a guy who was obviously looking for his room burst through the doorway. Who was more shocked, I never found out! The light awakened me, and I sat up feeling confused and surprised. We looked at each other, and he dived out the opposite doorway with an apology, "Sorry, lady, wrong room!"

Although I did manage to drift off to sleep again, unfortunately, it was not for long. On goes the light again, and the Manager's wife appears.

TYRE BLOWOUT

"Do you mind if this lady and her children share your room?" she asks. "There are no vacancies available, and we have put her husband in with a gentleman."

"Yes, that's okay," I stammer in my half-awake state, and there ensues an hour of preparation for bedtime while the children complain about sleeping in one bed and the exasperated mother whispers dire consequences if they continue to misbehave. I drift off to sleep again.

Next morning at the crack of dawn, after very little sleep, I crawl out of bed and head for the bathroom. There are a few grasshoppers left, so I bravely shower while I watch them, and they watch me! I am the first one down to breakfast, packed and ready to go.

That day during the return flight, after landing at Blackall, I needed to check the passenger list with the agent, so I walked across to where he was sorting luggage. That was when a host of brown grasshoppers converged on me, and as soon as I plucked one off my uniform, another one landed. They were everywhere, and the passengers waiting to board started clapping at my obvious discomfort.

"I'll bet these monsters are the ones that looked at me malevolently in the shower last night," I muttered as I quickened my pace back to the aircraft. Relieved to be safely inside the cabin I checked that refreshments had been loaded then waited for the passengers to board. As the last passenger steps in, he says with a smile, "I have something for you, hold out your hand."

Not to offend the passenger, I hold out my hand, and he drops a big, fat grasshopper into my palm. I am not one usually given to screaming, but I gave a low-key sound that resembled one and flung it out the door amidst much laughter from the passengers. That was a happy flight; we had a bond – a plague of fearsome grasshoppers. They can make a mess of an aircraft windscreen too!

CHAPTER 22

Dust Storm Over New South Wales

On the news not long ago, a TV station showed a red dust storm rolling in over the land like a huge red wave. It brought to mind a flight I crewed while on loan to Sydney port.

On this particular flight, the aircraft was a propeller-driven DC-4 Skymaster, which carried 44 passengers travelling in rows of double seats on either side of the cabin. Two pilots, a Captain and a First Officer, and two Air Hostesses. I enjoyed working on it because it was a larger version of the DC-3 and prone to similar flying conditions – the bumps and the unpredictable behaviour of the much-loved DC-3. It had four engines and was also unpressurised.

However, take off was different from the DC-3. It seemed ponderous and lumbering until it gathered speed and roared along the runway and became airborne. The flight was a direct Sydney/Adelaide, and we had a full load of passengers, so we knew we were going to be busy. Before taxiing out to the runway, after the cabin door was closed and

COME FLY WITH ME ... ON A DC-3

locked ready for departure, the pilots fired up each engine one by one. As they burst into life with a spluttering roar, a cloud of smoke gushed from behind each engine and this always alarmed passengers who were first-time flyers. Burning oil caused this smoke cloud and was nothing to worry about as it usually cleared after a minute or so of running.

We were well into the flight, conditions were smooth, and everyone was settled when, suddenly without warning, over western New South Wales near the South Australian border, we were enveloped in a red dust storm and buffeted by the wind gusts swirling around us. The cabin became infused with a red glow as though the storm was not only outside but inside as well. The Seatbelt sign came on, we cleared everything that could become a projectile, checked that passengers were strapped in and we sat down ourselves as the No Smoking sign was on too.

Unfortunately, it was a frightening experience for the junior hostess who was with me because the red glow and the hammering the aircraft was subjected to was probably a once in a lifetime incident. In a way, it was similar to flying through dense rain cloud in North Queensland during the wet season, when landing could take three-quarters of an hour while the pilots made an instrument let down.

The Captain buzzed, and I walked the aisle swaying from side to side, clutching the seat headrests for support, checking the passengers for signs of distress and reached the cockpit without mishap. Nothing could be seen through the windscreen except a red cloud mass. We were flying blind. The Captain explained our predicament and what it would entail, and I noticed he was wearing gloves. I had never seen a pilot wearing gloves before, and throughout my three years with TAA, I had never felt afraid when in difficult situations. I had complete trust in the pilots and their knowledge of how to handle hazardous flying conditions.

The passengers were very quiet while we flew through the dust storm. It must have been scary for them not knowing when we would break through into clearer skies. When at last we were greeted by blue sky, everyone started chattering, relieved we had come through safely.

When pilots are being checked by a check pilot, part of the procedure is to cover the windscreen so that they are flying blind and relying on instruments. I have seen that many times, so it was not a new experience for me; however, the dust storm was!

When we arrived at Adelaide Airport, we were told not to discuss the flight with the crowd of reporters gathered in the lounge area. I am sure they would have gleaned information from the disembarking passengers who were full of admiration for the pilots. To stay calm in a situation such as this is extremely important because the passengers usually follow your lead and if you project confidence and reassurance and always smile no matter what the circumstances, they will relax and not panic.

The return flight was calm, no dust storms hanging around to cause us worry.

CHAPTER 23

Tricks Of The Trade

"Joking is undignified: that is why it is so good for one's soul."

G.K. Chesterton (1874-1936) British Writer

The DC-4 is a four-engine (piston) propeller-driven airliner developed by the Douglas Aircraft Company.

While on loan to Sydney port I crewed several DC-4 Skymaster flights. On one particular flight, as we headed back to Sydney, the Captain asked, "Would you like to come up to the cockpit for landing, Joy?"

"Oh yes, I would, thank you," I replied, excited to have the opportunity to watch the landing procedures and the ultimate touchdown from the cockpit, something like a close encounter for me!

We cleared the buffet (two hosties on the DC-4), checked that all passengers were wearing seatbelts, and none were smoking, and up I went. I have to say I did not know whether to laugh or cry because on the approach the Captain kept muttering "Get down, you bitch, get down," and I fervently hoped "she" was going to respond as I could almost feel the weight of the aircraft. I was told later that the Captain was a bomber pilot during the Second World War (1939-1945) so I assumed he often used that expression. I gave him the benefit of the doubt and hoped he was not referring to me. Should I have been crouching? True or False?

There were a few practical jokers among the pilots, and I had to appreciate their sense of humour even though it was often at our expense.

On a particularly bumpy flight, I went up to the cockpit to collect the pilots' lunch trays. The First Officer was still eating his fruit salad (tinned – opened with the stab can opener!), so I left him with the bowl. Next visit when I collected the coffee mugs, I was surprised to find the First Officer throwing up into a sick bag. In rough flying conditions, fruit salad was well known as a vomit inducer, but the cockpit was a reasonably stable place on a DC-3, and it was the first time I had seen a pilot being airsick.

As we began our descent, I checked the passengers for seatbelts and headed into the cockpit to see if the First Officer needed ginger ale or water. Imagine my astonishment when I found him eating the regurgitated fruit salad from a brown paper bag, scooping it up with gusto with a white plastic spoon. Was I startled – no, shocked!

He folded the top down, turned to me and with a satisfied grin explained, "I was still hungry, and it was delicious, no use wasting good food," then he handed me the bag and the spoon. There were a few questioning glances from passengers as I walked down the cabin aisle for disposal of the bag. Do we have an airsick pilot? True or False?

On another western flight after numerous ports of call, we touched down at Blackall. I was standing at the cabin door waiting for the passengers to disembark when suddenly the First Officer miraculously appeared at the foot of the steps, tie askew, shirt tails hanging out, hat at a rakish angle and panting heavily, looking decidedly worse for wear as he staggered up the steps.

"You forgot me!" he panted, "you left me behind, and I had to run all the way to catch up!"

I was so astounded that I could not speak, but my brain was telling me, "Impossible." Had he climbed out of the cockpit window – his was the right-hand seat – hopped off the wing and run around the tail? I wondered what the passengers thought! True or false?

COME FLY WITH ME ... ON A DC-3

Cartoon of 'Pilot Left Behind', by artist Judy Clarke

One other flight I was clearing the buffet when the First Officer came down and entered the lavatory. Not long after the buzzer sounded, so I walked up to the cockpit, checking passengers on the way, entered and closed the door. Luckily it stayed closed because sometimes when it was bumpy, the door would swing open and the passengers had a bird's eye view of the pilots! They really enjoyed that insight!

TRICKS OF THE TRADE

On this particular day, I was glad the door was closed because the pilots' seats were empty. The aircraft was flying on auto. I stared at the empty seats for a minute, my mind confused momentarily, then common sense told me the Captain had to be somewhere in the cockpit, so I started checking the baggage compartment and yes – there he was trying to look inconspicuous underneath a pile of freight! True or False?

On a western flight, I was handing out magazines when a white-faced passenger grabbed my arm and in a shaky voice said, "Excuse me, that engine out there has stopped," and he pointed out the window.

My inspection of the engine through the passenger's window confirmed that we had indeed lost an engine so I looked at him, smiled and told him, "No need to worry, this aircraft can fly on one engine," at which he looked sceptical, not at all convinced.

"I am sure it can," I thought as I headed into the cockpit for reassurance. The Captain verified that it could fly on one engine, but we had an unscheduled overnight stay at the next port of call and the following day had a long wait for a replacement aircraft.

One of the highlights of my flying career as an Air Hostess was when the Captain decided to talk to the passengers and offered me his left-hand seat.

"You can fly the aircraft while I'm in the cabin, Joy."

"Oh no, I couldn't," I protested.

"Yes, you can, all you have to do is keep the artificial horizon level," and he pointed to the instrument panel, "besides, the First Officer will keep an eye on you. Climb in."

And, that is what I did, I climbed in, and for the whole time, I dare not let my eyes wander from the instruments. Total concentration! The slightest deviation port or starboard and I was on to it!

That day after the flight, I walked tall! True or false?

CHAPTER 24

A Four-day Western

One of the most interesting flights I was lucky enough to crew was a four-day western - Brisbane, Charleville, a station property, Birdsville, Leigh Creek, Charleville, Brisbane.

Some of the details elude me, but our first overnight was Corones Hotel, Charleville. Second overnight Birdsville Hotel, Birdsville then The Mine's Visitors Accommodation, Leigh Creek, back to Charleville overnight, on to Brisbane the next day.

I do remember landing at a remote station property on the second day of the flight and the lady of the house bringing a morning tea tray down to the edge of the strip not far from the homestead. What a surprise, delicious home-made biscuits and a huge tin pot of steaming tea. How gracious and how welcome, a real treat. After the pilots had unloaded fresh vegetables, mail, newspapers and machinery replacements, we sat on the side of the strip enjoying her hospitality and drinking tea from enamel mugs instead of our blue plastic cups we carried on the aircraft. A much better taste!

COME FLY WITH ME ... ON A DC-3

There were two young ladies staying at the homestead, and they asked the Captain if he would take them to Leigh Creek and back via Birdsville. It was a great opportunity for them to see that part of the country. They were very excited as we took off looking forward to an adventure and that night, we shared a room at the Birdsville Hotel. The room had whitewashed cement rendered walls that hosted innumerable huntsman spiders which crawled out under cover of darkness and scurried away at the slightest sound or movement. The lavatory was some distance from the main building, so I was glad of the girls' company, particularly at night for the long trek there and back. It was a tin shed with a timber seat cover over the stand above a deep hole in the ground.

"Please don't fall in," I cautioned the girls, "it is a long way down." We also checked for spiders and snakes. Mission accomplished, and I hoped I did not have to get up during the night and paddle all that way on my own.

After dinner, a drover and his dog slept on the back verandah of the hotel while his horse spent the night tied to a verandah post. A high wire fence surrounded the enclosure behind our room, and when I asked, "Why the wire barricade?" I was told by the manager, "To keep out the dingoes. There is a food store down the back."

Birdsville, in the Shire of Diamantina, was originally named The Diamantina Crossing and almost all of the town's (not a very big town) early buildings were built of local sandstone. It was later called Birdsville because of the birdlife.

The girls and I spent the afternoon with the two nurses at the Australian Inland Mission Hospital, now heritage listed. The single-storey building was erected in 1953 to replace the original which was burnt down in 1951.

The nurses were so glad to have some female company, and I had a turn on the pedal radio which was their main form of communication.

A FOUR-DAY WESTERN

Some of the tales they told us were amusing, some sad and some simply awe-inspiring. Because of the area's remoteness, these brave young women were often faced with complicated medical decisions, a responsibility not for the faint-hearted.

Leigh Creek, our next overnight, was a coal mining town north of Adelaide in Eastern Central South Australia and we spent an interesting afternoon checking out the state-of-the-art mine machinery.

Next morning as I prepared for our departure, I found that Catering had given me eggs for breakfast. My quandary was – how to cook them? There were no cooking facilities on the DC-3 and no saucepans in the Mines Accommodation small kitchen. Since I was heating hot water in the sink heater for the urn, I dropped them into the urn and crossed my fingers. All good, we ate boiled eggs and bread rolls for breakfast, plus cereal that we had loaded in Charleville. I will never know whether the eggs had already been cooked!

On the return trip we called into the station property to offload the girls, collected mail and parcels for posting, then took off waving goodbye to the girls who told us they enjoyed every minute of their unplanned adventure. Taking off from station strips is not the same as taking off from a smooth city runway. The ground is uneven, sheep, cattle and kangaroos often inhabit the strip and have to be driven off before take-off. It can be a bumpy experience and sometimes hazardous with rocks, potholes and plenty of red dust.

The next port of call and last overnight was Charleville. We were always well looked after at Corones Hotel and after a long hot bath and a good night's sleep we were in the air again and on the way back to Brisbane and home, ready for a couple of days off.

I consider myself very lucky to have been able to visit these remote places and meet the resilient, friendly people of the Outback, and the DC-3 never missed a beat.

COME FLY WITH ME ... ON A DC-3

A friend, Betty Clayton (Monteith) said, "We flew in such a challenging era...it was tough, and some girls could not cope, which was understandable. I still have great affection for those old DC-3 days."

So, what was the emotional pull the DC-3 had for air hostesses of the early 1950's? I have already said it was a reliable aircraft and battled courageously through all weather conditions. For me, I always felt safe, I never worried no matter how much turbulence followed us or waited for us sometimes with unrelenting fury, always testing the DC-3's endurance.

The unique sound of its engines has stayed with me over the years and like all hosties who flew in this intrepid aircraft it "left a footprint in my heart" like a true friend, a noble spirit.

When the Exhibition (The Ekka) came around in August each year, I carried many passengers who were enroute for a few days respite in Brisbane to check out agriculture, machinery, cattle, sheep, horses, sideshows and meet up with friends. On a couple of occasions, I had a full aircraft of passengers from Quilpie, Western Queensland. Each year, they very kindly invited me to join them for lunch at the hotel where they were staying. They were a friendly group; usually about 20 people or more, who were happy to be able to take some time off from their isolated properties and I always enjoyed myself in their company because they were easy-going and pampered me!

A FOUR-DAY WESTERN

The following joke is from AIRLINES, the newsletter of Wings Away (Qld) Inc. January 2015. It was sent to Laurel Fraser (Cray), edited by Marie Douglas (Errington) with her best wishes to members.

This is a true story of a poor dizzy blonde flying in a little aeroplane with just the pilot. He has a heart attack and dies. She, frantic, calls out a Mayday.

"Mayday! Mayday! Help me, my pilot has had a heart attack and is dead, and I don't know how to fly. Please help me!"

She hears a voice over the radio saying, "This is Air Traffic Control, and I have you loud and clear. I will talk you through this and get you back on the ground. I have had a lot of experience with this kind of problem. Now, just take a deep breath. Everything will be fine. Now give me your height and position!" She says, "I'm 5'4", and I'm in the front seat".

"OK," says the voice on the radio. "Repeat after me. Our Father who art in Heaven …"

COME FLY WITH ME ... ON A DC-3

**Birdsville Dunny courtesy of Glenis Thompson 1962
You can just make out two different levels of "DROP"
Lower level for "LITTLE" people other for "BIG" people.**

CHAPTER 25

I Copped The Lot!

We were on the return flight 467 after an overnight in The Isa landing at Cloncurry, Julia Creek, Richmond, Hughenden, Charters Towers, Townsville. It was mid-February, and the summer heat was intense. The DC-3 was continually buffeted by updrafts fed by the extreme ground heat, and the passengers were not travelling well. Airsickness was exacerbated by the fact that the distance between ports of call was reasonably short, so the pilots flew lower, thus eliminating time climbing and descending as they followed the railway line.

Descending into Hughenden on the hop from Richmond, the turbulence increased, so I checked that everyone was wearing seatbelts in compliance with the Fasten Seatbelt sign switched on by the pilots, utilising the time to collect used sick bags for disposal as I went. If the No Smoking sign had also been activated, I too would need to be strapped in. With everything ready for landing, I was standing at the rear of the cabin, in the gyrating tail, keeping an eye on the passengers when a man in a forward seat stood up.

He stumbled towards me clinging to the seats as his body swayed with the motion of the aircraft – I assumed he was heading for the lavatory. When he drew level with me and we were face-to-face, I asked, "Can I help you?" He opened his mouth to speak; regrettably no words escaped just a steady stream of vomit. I copped the lot!

"Please be seated," I gasped. "We will be landing soon. There are sick bags in the pocket of the seat in front of you."

Without a word, he turned and staggered back to his seat.

A bottle of soda water cleaned my uniform to some extent, even so, the smell lingered for the remainder of the flight and the tram ride home.

After landing at Hughenden, the passengers exited for a breath of fresh air, albeit hot air, and I was still cleaning my uniform when the pilots came down to check the uplift weight and the aircraft.

"What on earth happened to you, Joy?" asked the Captain.

"Oh, an accident. A passenger used me as a sick bag." I explained, trying to sound as though it did not really matter.

The Captain was furious on my behalf, and I heard him berating the passenger. "I have a good mind to leave you here, and you can find your own way home."

I felt sorry for the man who was looking embarrassed and made sure I smiled as I greeted him when he returned to the cabin. I put the incident behind me for the remainder of the flight; thankfully, it was the first and only time that sort of thing happened to me – I definitely did not need another!

CHAPTER 26

The Convair CV-240

"Half the joy in life is in the little things taken on the run."

Victor Cherbuliez.

I enjoyed crewing this twin-engine aircraft. It carried 40 passengers who were loaded through a stairway in the tail, and they were seated in double rows both port and starboard of the cabin. It was a clean aircraft in which to work, with two hostesses, usually a senior and a junior, who were easily identified by two pale blue stripes (senior) on summer uniform epaulettes or one stripe (junior). In the winter months, the sleeves of our suit coat displayed either two stripes or one stripe on each sleeve just above the wrist. We became seniors after flying for 18 months, which was a reasonable amount of time to prove one's worthiness, especially in Queensland.

Compared with our beloved DC-3, the Convair was a faster aircraft, pressurised, and cabin noise was quieter. Unfortunately, while based in Brisbane, I only crewed an occasional flight, a respite from the strenuous physical activity that faced us on the DC-3. However, on one flight, a Brisbane-Sydney-Brisbane direct, I suffered an accident on the Brisbane-Sydney leg.

The buffet was behind the cockpit, a comparatively small area, very neat and compact. I elected to do the "running" in the cabin while Sylvia prepared the trays. We had just about cleared the lunch trays when we struck turbulence, unusual at 32,000 feet. The Fasten Seatbelt sign came on so I immediately checked the passengers, removing cups, glasses anything that could become a projectile, while Sylvia made sure that everything in the buffet was locked down. As I walked down the aisle, I found a young girl, who was travelling alone, heaving into a sick bag, poor child, so I stood behind her seat, leaned over and held her forehead. At least she knew someone was helping.

Suddenly, the aircraft literally fell out of the sky. I was thrown against the ceiling of the cabin and came down flat on my back on the aisle floor with a leg over each armrest! Shocked and stunned for a few seconds I heard shouts and saw passengers climbing out of seats to help me, so I am lying there in a most undignified position calling out, "Everyone sit down. Everyone sit down!" and they did, they sat down. There was still some turbulence and a lot of chatter from the passengers as I finally extricated my legs and was able to stand, somewhat shaken. I had a swollen right knee, tattered stockings (no need to worry about seams being straight) and definitely a bruised ego! By this time, the young girl had stopped vomiting, which was a good sign, and eventually, everyone settled down. From this incident you can see how important it is to wear your seatbelt because we had no warning before we fell, everything happened quickly.

I asked Sylvia to tell the Captain what had happened as we were obliged to report any accidents and he said he would radio for an ambulance to meet the aircraft at Mascot Airport so that I could be checked before working the return trip as our flight was a turn-around. Despite the Sydney Hostess Supervisor wanting me to stay

THE CONVAIR CV-240

overnight in Sydney, I elected to crew the flight back to Brisbane, so TAA gave me three days off and paid for a medical consultation to check my knee.

What had happened, you might ask? A good question. The aircraft simply fell one thousand feet, and that is why I was thrown against the ceiling. The pilots crewing the flight above us in the opposite direction watched in disbelief as we plummeted and told us they said, "That's it, they've gone!" Miraculously, the fall was halted. A couple of days later, we were requested to write reports on the incident, but it was soon forgotten and never bothered me. It did not affect my love of flying.

On my first Convair flight, I elected to check the passengers boarding through the tail, so it was up to me to activate the stairway to make sure it did close and lock! This I did with some trepidation after being given the "all clear" from the Traffic Officer. Mesmerised, I watched the steps rise, and when they locked into place, and the red light from the cockpit glowed, I knew the tail stairway was locked. I had this dreadful thought that if the stairway fell open during flight, we would all be sucked out! Pure fantasy, of course.

Another instance, on loan to Sydney port, the Convair Captain asked me if I would like to come up to the cockpit for take-off. Yes! A great opportunity to see and feel the thrill of watching the runway disappear beneath us.

After all the cabin chores were completed and the second hostess was aware of where I would be for take-off, I reached the cockpit just as the pilots were completing their checking. The Captain looked at the First Officer and asked with raised eyebrows, "Shall we?" the First Officer nodded, and the question was answered. The take-off was almost vertical, and I was pinned against the bulkhead by the force. The pilots thought it was a huge joke, but it was an incredible experience, and I hoped the passengers enjoyed it too.

COME FLY WITH ME ... ON A DC-3

When I eventually transferred to Melbourne port towards the end of 1954, I crewed many Convair flights; however, no other aircraft replaced my affection for the incredible DC-3.

Photo of CONVAIR 240 provided by Warwick Henry, courtesy of John Wren TAA Museum

CHAPTER 27

Winter Months

"Memory is the treasury and guardian of all things."

Cicero

The glorious winter months in Queensland were conducive to smooth flying conditions. Clear blue sky, cold nights and mornings, warm days, a welcome respite from the exhausting heat of summer when flights were demanding, not only in the air but on the ground as well. It was a time for enjoying nature's way of resting the land and the people.

Gone were the days of standing at the cabin door and as passengers entered brushing their backs trying to dislodge the myriads of tenacious flies, even so, the cabin was soon inundated by the sticky little creatures. And no longer did we employ the bush salute, waving hands endlessly around our faces in case we swallowed one which is what I did once when riding a horse on our property at Gawler in South Australia! We carried fly spray in one of those old-fashioned pump cans, but I was reluctant to use it as I found, through experience, that the spray could incite air sickness in some passengers. The one thing I wanted to avoid was having passengers in my care puking; I preferred that they enjoy a relaxing and comfortable flying experience.

One of my favourite flights during winter was the overnight Longreach staying at the Imperial Hotel. Ports of call were Charleville, Blackall, Longreach. With only three landings, it was an easy flight, and if we arrived on time in Longreach, we could attend the open-air pictures and watch a film under the clear midnight blue sky where stars seemed more radiant and luminous than in the city. To combat the cold, we wore coats and covered our legs with rugs.

The next morning after breakfast we sat in the sun on the sheltered verandah outside our rooms (we were on the second storey) and enjoyed a quiet chat, a read or a doze, then when time to prepare for the return flight loomed I would head off to take a "smelly" shower – bore water, it smelled like rotten eggs, so I avoided breathing through my nose as much as possible, mostly taking gulps of air through my mouth. The good thing was the underground bore water was already heated, no need for electricity, a big saving on bills.

One of my friends, Mary Ellis (Quinn), sadly now deceased, often took her violin to Longreach and would play requests after dinner. The hotel guests really enjoyed the music for Mary was a gifted musician, both violin and piano and when, halfway through the evening, a guest would offer to buy her a drink, she would reply, "I only drink champagne!" So, champagne it was!

The Dry season in Darwin was also a great time to spend a few days staying at the Hotel Darwin. Mind you, days were still relatively hot, but nothing like the wet season. Times change and places change, but in the early 1950s, Darwin was a tropical paradise. Towns become cities, and with high rise buildings and suburban sprawl, the untamed beauty of Darwin has disappeared. The Top End has been modernised. Has it lost its enigma? For me – yes!

CHAPTER 28

The Russian Built DC-3 – Lisunov li-2

A total of 4,937 Lisunov Li-2's were built under licence from Douglas and these were issued in 1936. The Russians had to spend a great deal of time converting everything to metric sizes, and some other changes were made as well.

Over page is a photograph of a Lisunov Li-2 which I took at the Moscow Aircraft Museum when I was there a few years ago. You will notice that the front of the engines has "shutters" that could be moved from the cockpit. These were to prevent a build-up of snow in the front of the engines when parked in winter.

COME FLY WITH ME ... ON A DC-3

LISUNOV Li-2 courtesy of Frank Shipway

FRANK SHIPWAY
Airworthiness Inspector and Consultant

CHAPTER 29

Wings Away (Qld) Inc

Wings Away was formed in 1966 to provide the opportunity for former Air Hostesses of Trans-Australia Airlines (TAA) not only to renew old acquaintances and make new ones but to work together to raise funds to help physically and mentally disadvantaged children in Australia. As time went on this also included Hostesses/Flight Attendants from Australian Airlines and Qantas.

To date, Wings Away has raised more than $1.3 million, with each state choosing the charity they wished to support.

In 2016, we celebrated 50 years of Wings Away here in Brisbane with over 300 members from all over Australia gathering for four wonderful days of fun, friendship and reminiscing. At that time, all states, with the exception of Queensland, decided to close owing mainly to the age of members, but Queensland has remained viable, inviting members from other states to join us and continues to function with over 200 members.

We are still a vibrant club and, at this point in time, we support Tippy Toes in Brisbane, Sunshine Coast Children's Therapy Centre and

Arundel Riding School for the Disabled on the Gold Coast, as well as supporting individual needy children and their families. Last year we also donated to the Longreach Drought Appeal.

In terms of friendship, the value of Wings Away can never be over-estimated. The love of flying has bound us together with a chain that can never be broken. We look out for each other – there is no age barrier - in fact, one of our members began flying with TAA in 1946 and still attends our monthly meetings. It makes no difference whether you worked alone on a DC-3 in the Outback or joined with others to serve on the biggest jets.

We get together for a monthly meeting and luncheon and enjoy several fundraising activities during the year.

Former Air Hostesses and Flight Attendants interested in reconnecting with past colleagues and making new friends can contact Robyn Grant on (07) 3300 2280 or robann@powerup.com.au or Maureen Mosely on (07) 3325 2676 or mosely4035@gmail.com

MAUREEN MOSELY (COOPER)
EX TAA AIR HOSTESS (1963-1965)

While writing this article on Wings Away, a couple of flights came to mind. My most vivid memory is of the plane flying low and John Doyle opening the door and dropping the mail out to various cattle properties.

On another flight to Birdsville, Easter 1963, and after quite a lot of rain, I was amazed to see the waterways in the Channel Country. The

Captain on that flight was Captain Merv Thomas. I don't recall the name of the First Officer. As a young girl fresh out of Melbourne, this certainly opened my eyes to the enormity of the area of Queensland!

Another time, I was fortunate to crew a DC-3 flight to Richmond with a Lions Club and was invited to attend a Ball there that evening with the passengers. I accepted the invitation and thoroughly enjoyed the evening. Flying was certainly very different in those days!
MAUREEN MOSELY.

END

Author

*"Age only matters when one is ageing.
Now that I have arrived at a great age
I might just as well be twenty."*

Picasso

Joy Allardyce was born on Armistice Day, 11th November 1930 and named "Joy" because it symbolised the end of World War I carnage. She grew up in the Sydney suburb of Maroubra and, since early childhood, has been an avid reader. She danced for nine years - tap, ballet, Russian and Dutch, performing in clogs. She also learned the piano and had elocution and drama lessons.

Before joining Trans-Australia Airlines (TAA), she was private secretary to the Managing Director of Otis Elevators in Sydney. Her love of flying began in her teens when she flew as a passenger to Evans Head on her way to Nimbin on a DC-3 carrying, as cabin luggage, a large glass jar that contained goldfish for an aunt who lived in Evans Head (that would never be allowed now) and later to Tumut via Wagga Wagga, also on a DC-3, then to Hayman Island by flying boat taking off from Rose Bay, Sydney Harbour. She flew home from Hayman via Proserpine to Brisbane (TAA DC-3) and Brisbane to Sydney (Ansett DC-3).

Joy has had short stories, human-interest stories and poems published and worked for the West Australian newspaper in the 1970s while living in Mount Newman, Western Australia. That was after studying Professional Journalism through the Adelaide Technical College. In 1987, Joy was awarded the Year 12 English prize at the Queensland Secondary Correspondence School. Her speech was entitled "The Wonderful World of Literature". Since her three daughters have their own families and careers now, she calls her books her children!

Joy lives high on a hill overlooking the city of Toowoomba in Queensland. On the second Thursday of each month, she meets with other ex hosties for lunch, and besides enjoying each other's company, they have a few laughs and reminisce about "those good old flying days". The group consists of TAA, Ansett/ANA, Ansett and Qantas ex hosties. There is a special bond that exists between ex hosties who are always willing to help and support each other when the need arises.

If you wish to purchase this book, please email Joy Allardyce at: joyallardyce@gmail.com

Acknowledgements

"The woods are lovely, dark and deep,
But I have promises to keep,
And miles to go before I sleep,
And miles to go before I sleep."

"Stopping by woods on a snowy evening"
Robert Frost 1875 - 1963 USA

In the past, when I have submitted a manuscript for perusal, it has been on paper and forwarded by mail through the post! Now the publisher receives the manuscript via the computer. How things have changed! My sincere thanks to my daughter, Tracy, who encouraged me and taught me the necessary skills that enabled me to do just this. Your uncomplaining assistance is very much appreciated, especially since you were writing your own book at this time.

Regarding the early beginnings of Trans-Australia Airlines (TAA), I researched this in Sir Hudson Fish's "Wings to the World" which is the third book of a trilogy. I also acknowledge Nancy Bird Walton's "My God! It's a Woman" wherein she writes of her meeting with

COME FLY WITH ME ... ON A DC-3

Donald Douglas, "that genius of aviation" who was responsible for the manufacture and design of the DC-3.

I have quoted passages from my short story "...and the Flights Headed West" published in the Sunday Mail's colour magazine on December 16, 1979. I was living in Mount Isa in the 1970s and the environment sparked vivid memories of crewing the DC-3 out west – the heat, the dust and the flies!

My thanks to my daughter, Lindy, for her expertise on the idea for the book cover. After my futile attempts, you saved the day (in fact you have saved many days), and your IT knowledge often helped me out of sticky situations.

My grateful thanks to Air Hostesses Annie Butt, Anna Elliott, Laurel Fraser, Fleur Hanley, Barbara Hofmann, Fay Lambert, Maureen Mosely, Leonie Plummer and Glenis Thompson for your valuable contributions. To Pilot Rob Fraser, who never complained when I asked a question, and to Pilot Kerry Huston for sharing their love of flying DC-3's and to my cousin, Frank Shipway, Airworthiness Inspector and Consultant, who was always there for me, my heartfelt thanks. Thank you, Frank, for your photographs that bring the 1950's into the 2020's!

And, thank you to my daughter, Caroline, for her sketch of a DC-3 hot water urn. You were very patient because my memory of how the urns actually looked was a trifle hazy. If they are not true to character, I am the one to blame. How could I forget such an integral and essential component of the DC-3 cabin, one that tested my stamina every flight, not once but several times!

My thanks also to talented artist and good friend, Judy Clarke, for her cartoon illustrating 'the First Officer left behind' which definitely added humour to the book; after all, laughter is the best medicine. Judy said she has given us a pregnant kangaroo, a little joey on the way!

ACKNOWLEDGEMENTS

I researched Google for confirmation of my memories of both Leigh Creek and Birdsville, this certainly enhanced my knowledge of these two Outback towns. I still remember them as they were in 1953, sixty-six years ago when life was not so complicated, and we had time to appreciate the simple thigs in life.

The DC-3 image on the front cover and the inside of the front cover, is an image courtesy of AussieAirliners, thank you, Bob Smith. And to Brian Griffin, many thanks for the photograph of VH-AES "Hawdon" taken on the day of the re-enactment of TAA's first flight.

My grateful thanks to Natasa Denman, Ultimate World Publishing, for her encouraging comments during my book's journey.

And to all the lovely ladies, my ex hostie friends, who have supported and encouraged me, thank you for all the happy hours I have spent in your company, for the laughter and the camaraderie we have shared and will continue to share.

"Life is a marathon in which you reserve the sprint for the end. Mentally I pace myself. I have got an energy bank account and I can't afford to be overdrawn."

Peter Ustinov

COME FLY WITH ME ... ON A DC-3

This famous iconic poster of model, Nola Rose, portrays a TAA Air Hostess. The poster was introduced in 1954 and also used as a postcard, courtesy Trans-Australia Airlines and Australian Airlines. This poster was also used on a postage stamp included in "Nostalgic Advertisements" of famous Twentieth Century posters. Stamp and pack design by Sonia Young, Australia Post Design Studio.

www.ingramcontent.com/pod-product-compliance
Lightning Source LLC
Chambersburg PA
CBHW021151080526
44588CB00008B/296